Presented to:

Presented by:

Date:

Prayer is the breathing of the soul.

Project developed by Bordon Books, Tulsa, Oklahoma
Concept: Dave Bordon and Tom Winters
Project Writing: Gina Conroy, Cindy Sigler Dagnan, Belinda Mooney, and Donna Shepherd in association with SnapdragonGroupSM Editorial Services

Warner Faith
Hachette Book Group USA
1271 Avenue of the Americas, New York, NY 10020
Visit our Web site at www.warnerfaith.com

Printed in the United States of America
First Edition: November 2006
10 9 8 7 6 5 4 3 2 1

ISBN: 0-446-57935-1

# Anytime
# Prayers
FOR
# Everyday
# Moms

New York  Boston  Nashville

# Contents

# Prayers of Intercession . . . . . . . . . . . . . . . . . . . . . . . . . . . . . . . . .143

*Lifting My Voice to God on Behalf of Others*

**Prayers for my child:**

## Prayers for the world around us:

## Introduction

God wants to know you—and He wants you to know Him. It's a relationship He has invested His heart in. Does that surprise you? It shouldn't. You are God's most beloved creation, made in His own image. It's natural that He would want to communicate with you, and prayer is the means He has chosen to do just that.

Unfortunately, many people are intimidated by the idea of prayer. God seems so big, so powerful. Why would He care about our puny lives? Why would He want to hear about our troubles or heed our cries for help? The answers to those questions are beyond the scope of our limited understanding, but whatever His reasons, the Bible says He does—care, hear, and answer.

*Anytime Prayers for Everyday Moms* contains the prayers of women just like you—women who have ups and downs of every kind. It is our hope that as you pray along with them while reading the pages of this book, you will feel God's loving touch on your own life.

*O Precious Father, as we bow*
*Before Thy throne today—*
*We count the many blessings*
*Thou hast shower'd upon our way.*

Author Unknown

# Prayers of Praise and Thanksgiving

Lifting My Voice to God
for Who He Is and What He
Has Done for Me

# When I want to thank God
# for His abundance . . .

*God is able to provide you with every blessing in abundance,*
*so that by always having enough of everything, you may share*
*abundantly in every good work.*
2 CORINTHIANS 9:8 NRSV

*The LORD will establish you as his holy people . . .*
*if you keep the commands of the LORD your God and walk in*
*his ways. . . . The LORD will grant you abundant prosperity.*
DEUTERONOMY 28:9,11

*You crown the year with your bounty,*
*and your carts overflow with abundance.*
PSALM 65:11

*We went through fire and water,*
*but you brought us to a place of abundance.*
PSALM 66:12

*[O God,] you feed them from the*
*abundance of your own house.*
PSALM 36:8 NLT

# . . . I will pray.

Lord God,

Today I found myself falling into a familiar trap—complaining because for some reason I didn't think my family had enough. It's so easy for me to excuse my behavior. After all, what good mother doesn't desire the best for her children: the best housing, the best education, and the best clothes?

I wonder why I feel this way, but then I think of the advertisements bombarding me on every hand, touting newer and better products. Unfortunately, my children follow my lead—always wanting more. Even if my children had the best of everything, they would still be poor if they didn't praise You and realize that all blessings come from You. Lord, help me to teach my children that You promise to supply our needs and that we are to be thankful for all You give us.

And most of all, help us to stay mindful that You gave the best—Your Son, Jesus. Thank You for Your abundant grace. Father, I ask You to forgive me for those times when I forget that You not only supply all of my needs with abundance, but You shower additional blessings on us every day. I praise and thank You, God.

Amen.

God is absolutely unlimited in His ability and His resources. And He is unlimited in His desire to pour out those resources upon us.

Gloria Copeland

# When I want to thank God for His blessings . . .

[The Lord says] I will make them and the places around
My hill a blessing. And I will cause showers to come down
in their season; they will be showers of blessing.

EZEKIEL 34:26 NASB

Blessings are on the head of the righteous.

PROVERBS 10:6 RSV

The faithful will abound with blessings.

PROVERBS 28:20 NRSV

I, the LORD, am the one who answers your prayers and
watches over you. . . . Your blessings come from me.

HOSEA 14:8 NCV

If we are God's children, we will receive
blessings from God together with Christ.

ROMANS 8:17 NCV

# . . . I will pray.

Dear Lord,

Before we eat, our family says a prayer, thanking You for our food. If we started to give You praise for all the things You have blessed us with, we would be sitting at the table for hours! You have given us so much: life, each other, friends, possessions, and most of all, Your love. Your love provided for our salvation, and You take care of all of our needs through Your infinite resources.

Because You have been so good to me, my prayer today is that I will be faithful to share Your goodness with my children. I pray that I will be an example before them of someone who gives liberally. Lord, help me to be faithful in modeling an attitude of gratitude. I want to bless You with my praise and love.

I pray that I will focus on Your goodness and blessings first and foremost every time I pray.

Thank You, Lord, for the many ways You have showered our family with blessings.

Amen.

Reflect upon your present blessings
of which every man has many;
not on your past misfortunes
of which all men have some.

Charles Dickens

# When I want to thank God for His creative genius . . .

*God created man in His own image, in the image of God*
*He created him; male and female He created them.*
GENESIS 1:27 NASB

*Each of you must take responsibility for doing the creative*
*best you can with your own life.*
GALATIANS 6:5 MSG

*We are His workmanship, created in Christ Jesus for good*
*works, which God prepared beforehand so that*
*we would walk in them.*
EPHESIANS 2:10 NASB

*You made all the delicate, inner parts of my body, and*
*knit them together in my mother's womb. Thank you for*
*making me so wonderfully complex! It is amazing to think*
*about. Your workmanship is marvelous*
*—and how well I know it.*
PSALM 139:13-14 TLB

*Live creatively, friends.*
GALATIANS 6:1 MSG

# . . . I will pray.

O Lord,

Sometimes I get so frustrated with a world that tries to explain away Your creative power. When I see my children, I know only a magnificent God could have created such masterpieces. It's almost too much for me to comprehend when I think that there is no other being like them.

When I look at Your handiwork, I can't help but praise Your name. I see such promise in their faces. Will one be a doctor? Another a scientist? A mom like me? You knew my children before they came into this world, and You know the paths they will take.

All of my children are incredibly creative. We've had so much fun painting pictures and modeling clay. I overhear them putting on plays and singing little ditties they've composed. Lord, help me to nurture their appreciation for art, music, and literature, but most of all, may they always recognize that You are the Source of their creativity. Thank You for sharing Your creative genius with us.

Amen.

God is our Creator.
God made us in his image and likeness.
Therefore we are creators. . . .
The joy of creativeness should be ours.

Dorothy Day

# When I want to thank God for His faithfulness . . .

*Even when we are too weak to have any faith left,*
*[Christ] remains faithful to us and will help us,*
*for he cannot disown us who are part of himself,*
*and he will always carry out his promises to us.*
2 TIMOTHY 2:13 TLB

*I face your Temple as I worship, giving thanks to you for all*
*your lovingkindness and your faithfulness, for your promises*
*are backed by all the honor of your name.*
PSALM 138:2 TLB

*All the paths of the LORD are steadfast love and faithfulness,*
*for those who keep his covenant and his testimonies.*
PSALM 25:10 RSV

✿

*Your love, O LORD, reaches to the heavens,*
*your faithfulness to the skies.*
PSALM 36:5

# . . . I will pray.

Faithful Father,

When my children make promises, I can't always count on them. Broken promises have sometimes resulted in a broken heart, and in the darkest nights, I have cried out to You.

But Lord, You are faithful to keep Your promises. You've promised You will never leave me, and I know You cannot fail. When I call on You, I sense Your presence as You fill my soul with peace. I want to be Your faithful child—someone You can count on, because I know I can count on You anytime, every time, all the time.

When my children cause my world to tremble, I run to You. You're my Rock that cannot be shaken, and I put my trust in You.

God, even when my children try me to my limit, I'll be faithful to love them and let them know that they can depend on me. I'll remind them that You will never let them down. Help me as I teach them what it means to be faithful in all things, especially in their relationship with You.

Thank You for Your never-ending faithfulness to us.

Amen.

God's investment in us is so great
he could not possibly abandon us.

Erwin W. Lutzer

# When I want to thank God for His forgiveness . . .

*[Jesus said] Our Father in heaven . . . forgive us our sins,*
*just as we have forgiven those who have sinned against us.*
MATTHEW 6:9,12 TLB

*If You, LORD, should mark iniquities,*
*O Lord, who could stand?*
*But there is forgiveness with You.*
PSALM 130:3-4 NASB

✿

*Bear with each other and forgive whatever grievances*
*you may have against one another. Forgive as*
*the Lord forgave you.*
COLOSSIANS 3:13

✿

*Forgive one another as quickly and thoroughly as*
*God in Christ forgave you.*
EPHESIANS 4:32 MSG

✿

*[Jesus said] When you stand praying, if you hold anything*
*against anyone, forgive him, so that your Father in heaven*
*may forgive you your sins.*
MARK 11:25

# . . . I will pray.

O Lord,

How I wish I were the perfect person and mother all the time! This morning I made such a mistake. My frazzled nerves got to me, and I spoke harshly to my children—acting without thinking.

God, when I asked my children for their forgiveness, they responded with hugs and kisses, wrapping their arms around me to let me know that they forgave me.

It reminded me of the way I run to You when I need to be forgiven. You look into my heart and know my repentance is genuine. God, You wait for me with open heart and arms, ready to love and forgive. You even forget my offenses! May I be so gracious with my family and friends. I can be quick to anger but slow to pardon. As You forgive me, help me to forgive others in the same way.

May our family be quick to forgive and quick to restore peace. May Your love abound in each of us and be reflected in our words and deeds.

Thank You for the gift of forgiveness.

Amen.

When God pardons, he consigns the offense
to everlasting forgetfulness.

Merv Rosell

# When I want to thank God for His generosity . . .

*A generous person will be enriched,*
*and one who gives water will get water.*
PROVERBS 11:25 NRSV

*Whoever sows sparingly will also reap sparingly,*
*and whoever sows generously will also reap generously.*
*Each man should give what he has decided in his heart to*
*give, not reluctantly or under compulsion,*
*for God loves a cheerful giver.*
2 CORINTHIANS 9:6-7

*Good men will be generous to others and*
*will be blessed of God for all they do.*
ISAIAH 32:8 TLB

*It is good to be merciful and generous.*
*Those who are fair in their business*
*will never be defeated.*
*Good people will always be remembered.*
PSALM 112:5-6 NCV

# . . . I will pray.

Dear Father,

I've always tried to teach my children to be cheerful givers. My heart melted this morning when I saw my daughter offer her favorite toy to her crying baby sister. Thank You, Lord.

You alone are the Source of all our blessings, and I thank You for the gifts of life, salvation, and daily provisions. But, God, You are faithful to do more than I expect or can even imagine, and Your goodness goes far beyond what we deserve.

I want to teach my children that generosity encompasses more than finances. Help us to give of our time, our money, and ourselves. I pray my children will never become stingy but will realize that everything they have comes from You.

Lord, I want to be an example to my children of a generous, loving mother. You've promised that when we give, You return blessings to us many times over, and I've always found You faithful to keep that promise.

My prayer today is that my children become generous individuals who are willing to share the greatest blessing of all—Your love. Thank You for Your abundant generosity.

Amen.

If God is God, he's big and generous and magnificent.

J. B. Phillips

# When I want to thank God for His gifts . . .

*Behold, children are a gift of the* LORD,
*The fruit of the womb is a reward.*
PSALM 127:3 NASB

❀

*[Jesus said] If you sinful people know how to give
good gifts to your children, how much more will your
heavenly Father give good gifts
to those who ask him.*
MATTHEW 7:11 NLT

❀

*The wages of sin is death,
but the free gift of God is eternal life in
Christ Jesus our Lord.*
ROMANS 6:23 NASB

❀

*By grace you have been saved through faith;
and this is not your own doing, it is the gift of God.*
EPHESIANS 2:8 RSV

❀

*Every good action and every perfect gift is from God.*
JAMES 1:17 NCV

# . . . I will pray.

Father God,

You know I love celebrating birthdays. I look forward to giving and receiving gifts. On some occasions, I receive things that disappoint me. Some clothes don't fit or the color doesn't suit me, and I return or exchange many gifts.

But, Lord, when I look into the eyes of my children, I cannot believe You have blessed me so. Motherhood—what a gift! I know that nothing I have ever done could have merited such an honor. I experience Your love each time I hold my children, and as they snuggle into my arms, I thank You over and over again.

Oh, Lord, thank You that because You love us, You sent Your Son as a baby—the gift that meets everyone's needs, will never wear out, never break or need repairing. God, material items can never satisfy my spiritual hunger, but Your love overwhelms me and never disappoints.

Keep me mindful that all good things come from You. My children are priceless treasures, and I pray, God, that one day, they will accept Your salvation—a gift that lasts for eternity. Thank You for all Your gracious gifts.

Amen.

God is so good that he only awaits our desire to overwhelm us with the gift of himself.

François Fénelon

# When I want to thank God for His goodness . . .

*"Why do you ask me about what is good?" Jesus replied.*
*"There is only One who is good."*
Matthew 19:17

*I am still confident of this:*
*I will see the goodness of the* Lord
*in the land of the living.*
Psalm 27:13

*How great is your goodness,*
*which you have stored up for those who fear you,*
*which you bestow in the sight of men*
*on those who take refuge in you.*
Psalm 31:19

*In his goodness he chose to make us his own children by*
*giving us his true word. And we, out of all creation,*
*became his choice possession.*
James 1:18 nlt

# . . . I will pray.

Dear Father,

When my children behave, I tell them what good children they are. But, Lord, I know a radical difference exists between the way You see things and the way I do.

In truth, I realize nothing good exists in us outside of You. Your kindness shows in Your everyday dealings with me. I trust that You will direct the events taking place in the lives of my children as well. I know that all things work for good because You love us.

Everything I've achieved and all I possess come from Your hand. Lord, forgive me when I take the glory for any of my blessings. I never want to forget Your goodness in my life. I can't produce goodness. At times, I might look good in comparison to others, but I don't when I compare myself to Your perfection. Even at my best, I fall far short of that. The greatest kindness You've shown to us is sending Jesus to die on the cross for our sins.

Lord, help me teach my children about Your grace that provides our salvation and the only true goodness that comes from following Christ. Thank You for being such a good God.

Amen.

The Lord's goodness surrounds us at every moment.
I walk through it almost with difficulty,
as through thick grass and flowers.

R. W. Barbour

# When I want to thank God for His grace . . .

*From his fullness we have all received, grace upon grace.*
*The law indeed was given through Moses; grace and*
*truth came through Jesus Christ.*
JOHN 1:16-17 NRSV

*Even though on the outside it often looks like things are*
*falling apart on us, on the inside, where God is making new*
*life, not a day goes by without his unfolding grace.*
2 CORINTHIANS 4:16 MSG

*The amazing grace of the Master, Jesus Christ,*
*the extravagant love of God, the intimate friendship of the*
*Holy Spirit, be with all of you.*
2 CORINTHIANS 13:14 MSG

*If your life honors the name of Jesus, he will honor you.*
*Grace is behind and through all of this, our God giving*
*himself freely, the Master, Jesus Christ, giving himself freely.*
2 THESSALONIANS 1:12 MSG

# . . . I will pray.

Dear Lord,

It seems everything in this world depends on gaining favor. If I want a promotion, I garner the favor of my boss. My son has come home disappointed because he didn't gain the approval of a coach.

I'm thankful, God, Your love for us is not dependent on whether we're starting players in the eyes of the world. In Your eyes, our value does not vary in proportion. Our value is not even dependent on how good we are or upon how bad we have been. We are all of infinite value, and for that, I am grateful.

Understanding and accepting the fact that I need a Savior humbles me. Lord, despite my unworthiness, You love me. I find great comfort in knowing my children are of infinite worth in Your eyes and that You grace us with new life in Jesus Christ when we make You Lord of our lives.

I pray my children will accept Your favor and realize just how amazing grace is. Help us to see ourselves as You see us and to measure our value the way You do. Your grace still amazes me. Thank You for it.

Amen.

Grace is given not because we have done good works,
but in order that we may be able to do them.

Saint Augustine of Hippo

# When I want to thank God for His joy . . .

*Be full of joy in the Lord always.*
*I will say again, be full of joy.*
PHILIPPIANS 4:4 NCV

✿

*Consider it wholly joyful . . . whenever you are enveloped in*
*or encounter trials of any sort. . . . Understand that the trial*
*and proving of your faith bring out endurance and*
*steadfastness and patience.*
JAMES 1:2-3 AMP

✿

*[Nehemiah said] Do not be grieved,*
*for the joy of the LORD is your strength.*
NEHEMIAH 8:10 NASB

✿

*[The Lord says] The joy of the LORD will fill you to*
*overflowing. You will glory in the Holy One of Israel.*
ISAIAH 41:16 NLT

✿

*We are praying . . . that you will be filled with his mighty,*
*glorious strength so that you can keep going no matter what*
*happens—always full of the joy of the Lord.*
COLOSSIANS 1:11 TLB

# . . . I will pray.

Dear Lord,

During the Christmas holidays, we talk about joy often, but what joy we have all the time when we praise You! Children delight in happy times, giggling and enjoying life. Lord, I ask for that same carefree joy I felt as a child when my dad pushed me on the swing or Mom made homemade ice cream. Lord, put a song like that in my heart today.

Being a mother might be a challenge, but I desire to be a mother who can rejoice in the midst of difficult circumstances. Even when situations seem to be more than I can endure, help me to celebrate that You will be faithful to take me through.

Nothing compares to the simple joys of motherhood: first steps, the first day of school. I realize that though happiness may be fleeting, the joy that comes from You is my strength. And since You have given it to me, nothing can take it away.

Help me to experience and share with my children the deep, divine joy of Christmas all year long. Thank You for it.

Amen.

I have no understanding of a long-faced Christian.
If God is anything, he must be joy.

Joe E. Brown

# When I want to thank God for His love . . .

*This is what real love is: It is not our love for God;*
*it is God's love for us in sending his Son to be the way to*
*take away our sins.*
1 JOHN 4:10 NCV

*God's love has been poured into our hearts through*
*the Holy Spirit which has been given to us.*
ROMANS 5:5 RSV

*If anyone obeys his word, God's love is truly made*
*complete in him. This is how we know we are in him.*
1 JOHN 2:5

*May the Lord lead your hearts into God's love.*
2 THESSALONIANS 3:5 NCV

*God's love will continue forever.*
PSALM 52:1 NCV

# . . . I will pray.

O God,

Everything I do as a mother is motivated by my devotion to my children. My love for them seems limitless. It deepens and grows every day. Sometimes I sneak into their rooms at night just to look at them. As I gaze upon their sleeping faces, my chest swells with pride and my heart flutters with emotions too difficult to describe.

I love my children with all that's within me, but my love still does not compare to Yours. God, You are love. Your love for us is greater, deeper, and more powerful than even a mother's love. Your love is boundless and eternal.

Each day, I demonstrate my love for my children in many ways. I provide for them and take care of their needs. Lord, You showed Your great love for us when You provided for our salvation through Jesus Christ. Your amazing love brings us back into relationship with You, and I am so grateful.

Lord, I ask that You enable me to be a loving mother—a mother who demonstrates Your character. Thank You, God, for loving us.

Amen.

God does not love us because we are valuable.
We are valuable because God loves us.

Archbishop Fulton J. Sheen

# When I want to thank God for His mercy . . .

*All those who know your mercy, Lord, will count on you for*
*help. For you have never yet forsaken those who trust in you.*
PSALM 9:10 TLB

*I will always trust in you and in your mercy and*
*shall rejoice in your salvation. I will sing to the Lord because*
*he has blessed me so richly.*
PSALM 13:5-6 TLB

❖

*Generous in love—God, give grace!*
*Huge in mercy—wipe out my bad record.*
PSALM 51:1 MSG

❖

*God is sheer mercy and grace;*
*not easily angered, he's rich in love.*
PSALM 103:8 MSG

❖

*You can't whitewash your sins and get by with it;*
*you find mercy by admitting and leaving them.*
PROVERBS 28:13 MSG

# . . . I will pray.

Dear God,

Thank You so much for the opportunity You gave me this morning to teach my child. When my little one disobeyed me, punishment would have been justified. For some reason—was it You coaxing me along?—I decided instead to talk about the concept of mercy.

Lord, mercy is an aspect of Your character I cannot fully grasp. Our sin is great, but Your mercy is greater. Lord, I have a relationship with You only by Your compassion. You don't treat me the way I deserve to be treated. Thank You, God!

This morning when I pardoned the offense, my child stared at me, bewildered. As I attempted to explain, I realized I can't ever fully understand the great love that forgave me for my sin. Lord, I ask for wisdom as I continue to teach my children.

Help me to be merciful to others. Show me what I can do today to reflect that attribute. Open the door today that I might show my children how to extend great kindness by giving to others as You've given to us. Thank You for Your mercy, Lord.

Amen.

Our faults are like a grain of sand beside the great mountain of the mercies of God.

Saint Jean Baptiste Marie Vianney

# When I want to thank God for His patience . . .

*The Lord is not slow about His promise, as some count slowness, but is patient toward you, not wishing for any to perish but for all to come to repentance.*
2 PETER 3:9 NASB

*God had mercy on me, so that Christ Jesus could use me as a prime example of his great patience with even the worst sinners.*
1 TIMOTHY 1:16 NLT

*The fruit of the Spirit is . . . patience.*
GALATIANS 5:22 NASB

✿

*With patience you can convince a ruler, and a gentle word can get through to the hard-headed.*
PROVERBS 25:15 NCV

✿

*The patient in spirit is better than the proud in spirit.*
ECCLESIASTES 7:8 RSV

# . . . I will pray.

O Lord,

It's been one of those days. Sometimes I feel in such short supply of one trait a mother needs most—patience. I love my children with all my heart and would give my life for them, but my patience runs thin at times. I need Your help! I don't want my children to remember their mom as a harsh woman with a short fuse.

Hardly a day goes by that a situation doesn't arise to try me, Lord, and I take a deep breath and cry out to You. Who knew when I first became a mother that there would be days when I'd be at my wits' end?

But of course You knew. From the second You first breathed life into humankind, You've been long-suffering. You have untold patience with Your children when, some days, I have so little with mine. When I became a mother, You knew there'd be times I'd fall on my knees to call on You. I pray for a healthy dose of patience and kindness.

God, I thank You for Your patience. Show me Your ways, and help me to be like You. Thank You, Father.

Amen.

God's love for poor sinners is very wonderful,
but God's patience with ill-natured saints
is a deeper mystery.

Henry Drummond

# When I want to thank God for His peace . . .

*Don't worry about anything; instead, pray about everything;*
*tell God your needs and don't forget to thank him for his*
*answers. If you do this you will experience God's peace,*
*which is far more wonderful than the human mind can*
*understand. His peace will keep your thoughts and your*
*hearts quiet and at rest as you trust in Christ Jesus.*
PHILIPPIANS 4:6-7 TLB

✿

*[Jesus said] I am leaving you with a gift—peace of mind and*
*heart! And the peace I give isn't fragile like the peace the*
*world gives. So don't be troubled or afraid.*
JOHN 14:27 TLB

✿

*Following after the Holy Spirit leads to life and peace.*
ROMANS 8:6 TLB

✿

*Let the peace of heart which comes from Christ be always*
*present in your hearts and lives, for this is your responsibility*
*and privilege as members of his body.*
*And always be thankful.*
COLOSSIANS 3:15 TLB

# . . . I will pray.

O Lord,

Sometimes peace is hard to come by. Today I listened to cranky children whine and complain, with intermittent fights and screaming matches. The television blared out the latest news—all bad. After glimpsing the latest crisis flashing across the screen, my mind worked overtime as I began to worry. What is this world coming to?

Even in the middle of the night, obligations and concerns for my family's welfare call my name, demanding my attention. I find it difficult to settle into Your presence and find peace.

Lord, You are my refuge. Just as I gather my children close to my heart, I draw close to You. I want to hear Your heartbeat. I don't seek peace, but I seek You—the Giver of peace. In times of adversity, I trust Your plan. You are never late, never early, but always on time. When You become the center of my family, we will have peace at our core. I have full confidence in You, Lord. You will be with me, calming me as I rest in Your presence. Thank You for Your peace.

Amen.

❦

Finding God, you have no need to seek peace,
for he himself is your peace.

Frances J. Roberts

# When I want to thank God for His presence . . .

*God has made you his friends again. He did this through Christ's death in the body so that he might bring you into God's presence as people who are holy.*
COLOSSIANS 1:22 NCV

✿

*Be still in the presence of the LORD, and wait patiently for him to act.*
PSALM 37:7 NLT

*Wonderful times of refreshment will come from the presence of the Lord.*
ACTS 3:20 NLT

✿

*I was filled with delight day after day, rejoicing always in his presence.*
PROVERBS 8:30

✿

*Let us come before His presence with thanksgiving.*
PSALM 95:2 NKJV

# . . . I will pray.

Precious Lord,

When we went outside today, my daughter spread out a blanket, stretched out, and basked in the sunlight. She turned her face heavenward and sighed as the warmth permeated her body.

That's how I feel when I come into Your presence. The warmth of Your love permeates my spirit, and I can't help but turn my face heavenward.

I pray to You today because I know You listen. I find such comfort in knowing that You hear me. You are as near as my next breath and with me every moment of every night and day. O Lord, I give You control of my life.

Even when I don't acknowledge You, I know You are always there, working on my behalf, working things out for my good. Even when bad things happen in this life, I come to You for comfort and help.

Lord, help me to instill an awareness of Your presence in my children. Remind them to call on You when they are in distress or difficult situations arise—whether it's a bruised knee or a broken heart—and to praise You at all times. Thank You for Your abiding presence.

Amen.

As his child, you are entitled to his kingdom,
The warmth, the peace, and the power
of his presence.

Author Unknown

# When I want to thank God for His protection . . .

The LORD loves the just
and will not forsake his faithful ones.
They will be protected forever.
PSALM 37:28

Happy are those who trust him for protection.
PSALM 2:12 NCV

Let all who take refuge in you be glad;
let them ever sing for joy.
Spread your protection over them,
that those who love your name may rejoice in you.
PSALM 5:11

He shall give His angels charge over you,
To keep you in all your ways.
PSALM 91:11 NKJV

# . . . I will pray.

Dear God,

As I look out the window at my children waiting for the school bus, I feel panic deep within my soul. So many dangers lurk in this world, and as a mother, I want to gather my children into my arms to protect them. I feel so powerless to defend them. They jump out of bed and hit the floor running. Seldom do they give a thought to their safety. But I have to confess I have lain awake some nights, picturing the worst.

Lord, forgive me for not trusting You. You planned the days of my children's lives even before they were born, and You love them even more than I do—although I must admit that seems impossible.

I'll do my best to trust You to take care of them. I ask that You send Your strongest angels to keep watch over them and keep them safe. Lord, give me peace and help me to trust You more each day. Hold us in the palm of Your hand.

Thank You for Your strong arm that protects my family. Amen.

Angels are God's secret service agents.
Their assignment—our protection.

Meriwether Williams

# When I want to thank God for His provision . . .

*My God shall supply all your need according to*
*his riches in glory by Christ Jesus.*
PHILIPPIANS 4:19 KJV

✿

*[Jesus said] Don't worry about food—what to eat and drink;*
*don't worry at all that God will provide it for you. All*
*mankind scratches for its daily bread, but your heavenly*
*Father knows your needs. He will always give you all you*
*need from day to day if you will make the Kingdom of God*
*your primary concern.*
LUKE 12:29-31 TLB

✿

*You provided in Your goodness for the poor, O God.*
PSALM 68:10 NASB

✿

*He provides food for those who fear him;*
*he is ever mindful of his covenant.*
PSALM 111:5 RSV

✿

*He provided redemption for his people.*
PSALM 111:9

# . . . I will pray.

Heavenly Father,

It's tempting to think that because I work hard, I am always able to provide for our needs, but really, that is out of my control. Only You can orchestrate circumstances so that we always have enough.

I confess, Lord, to wanting a newer car, a bigger house, and nicer clothes. But when I think about it, I don't really need those things. I realize that if I live my life with an attitude that Your provision is not adequate, I'll always be searching for something more. God, forgive me for when I've been discontent. What example am I setting for my children? You've been so good to us.

When I depend on You, Your provision always meets our needs, usually with some left over. You know our requests even before we ask, and You already have the provision ready for us. Although I'm thankful for all You provide, most of all I'm thankful that You provided a Savior for our salvation.

I will be grateful and satisfied with Your provision, Lord, and I'll be more faithful to thank You in the presence of my children.

Amen.

He who gives us teeth will give us bread.

Jewish Proverb

# When I want to thank God for His salvation . . .

*The LORD lives, and blessed be my rock;*
*And exalted be the God of my salvation.*
PSALM 18:46 NASB

*[Peter said] Jesus is the only One who can save people.*
*His name is the only power in the world that has been given*
*to save people. We must be saved through him.*
ACTS 4:12 NCV

*I am not ashamed of the gospel: it is the power of God for*
*salvation to every one who has faith.*
ROMANS 1:16 RSV

*I tell you, now is the time of God's favor,*
*now is the day of salvation.*
2 CORINTHIANS 6:2

*If you confess with your mouth the Lord Jesus*
*and believe in your heart that God has raised Him*
*from the dead, you will be saved.*
ROMANS 10:9 NKJV

# . . . I will pray.

Lord God,

I got so exasperated this morning when my child rushed by, knocking over my favorite vase and smashing it to pieces far too tiny to put back together.

As I gathered up the pieces, I thought of how thankful I am that You don't look at our broken lives and decide we're beyond repair. When we call on You, You save us and make us whole again. Even when we're broken and shattered, You make us into a new creation.

I have such great love for my children, but You love them even more than I do. When they need something, I do my best to provide for that need; but, Father, You saw our greatest need and provided for our salvation. Thank You for the love of Christ, that He sacrificed His life for us.

Father, help me to live in such a way that my children will want to accept Christ as Savior. The greatest joy of my life would be to see my children accept Him and make Him the Lord of their lives. Thank You for salvation.

Amen.

Salvation is a gift you can ask for.

Author Unknown

# When I want to thank God for His wisdom . . .

*God's wisdom is deep, and his power is great.*
JOB 9:4 NCV

*Fools think their own way is right,*
*but the wise listen to advice.*
PROVERBS 12:15 NRSV

*Real wisdom, God's wisdom, begins with a holy life and is*
*characterized by getting along with others. It is gentle and*
*reasonable, overflowing with mercy and blessings, not hot one*
*day and cold the next, not two-faced.*
JAMES 3:17 MSG

*Wisdom will make your life pleasant*
*and will bring you peace.*
*As a tree produces fruit, wisdom gives life to those who use it,*
*and everyone who uses it will be happy.*
PROVERBS 3:17-18 NCV

# . . . I will pray.

Heavenly Father,

Countless guides exist to help me in my role as a mother. In every magazine, lists of tips tell readers the best way to raise their children. But that knowledge isn't enough and my own seems so limited, so I call on You for wisdom to deal with every situation that comes up. Oh, Father, I need wisdom beyond my own to make decisions.

As a parent, I value knowledge. I do my best to help my children do homework and acquire an education, but more importantly, I strive to teach them right from wrong and to love You and others.

When I'm uncertain in my choices, Father, give me wisdom. Help me to balance knowledge and experience with common sense and insight that come from You. Instruct me in Your way. You are my Guide—not only on this path of motherhood, but through life. When I listen to You, I'm assured my path will be made straight and my steps sure, for You know the way, and You travel with me.

Thank You, Father, for Your wisdom.

Amen.

Most of us go through life praying a little,
planning a little, . . . hoping but never being
quite certain of anything, and always secretly afraid
that we will miss the way. . . . There is a better way.
It is to repudiate our own wisdom and take instead
the infinite wisdom of God.

A. W. Tozer

Were half the breath that's vainly spent,
To heaven in supplication sent,
Our cheerful song would oftener be,
"Hear what the Lord has done for me."

Garnet Rolling

# Prayers of Supplication

Lifting My Voice to God
When I Need Help

# When I need a change of attitude toward my child . . .

May God, who gives this patience and encouragement,
help you live in complete harmony with each other—each
with the attitude of Christ Jesus toward the other.
ROMANS 15:5 NLT

Be made new in the attitude of your minds; and . . .
put on the new self, created to be like God in true
righteousness and holiness.
EPHESIANS 4:23-24

The word of God is living and active. . . .
It judges the thoughts and attitudes of the heart.
HEBREWS 4:12

A relaxed attitude lengthens life.
PROVERBS 14:30 NLT

The Kingdom of God is not a matter of what we eat or
drink, but of living a life of goodness and peace and joy in the
Holy Spirit. If you serve Christ with this attitude,
you will please God.
ROMANS 14:17-18 NLT

# . . . I will pray.

Lord God,

Usually I love being a mom, but lately my child has developed such an attitude—and it's not a pleasant one. Unfortunately, this new disposition brings out the worst in me. I'm ashamed when I don't display the maturity I should as a mother. I have a tendency to make excuses for my behavior, and that just compounds the problem. During times like these, You and I both know I could use an attitude adjustment.

I can empathize with my child because I remember my own childhood. And I realize that I am Your child and You are so patient with me. Remind me to pass this patience on to my young one, and help me to have a godly attitude—even in the midst of temper tantrums and pouting spells. Lord, help me to control my temper so I can respond with Your love. Give me wisdom to deal with my child's attitude and the strength to discipline the way You instruct.

And one last thing: help me to remember what a privilege it is to be a mom. Thank You for helping me keep a positive attitude.

Amen.

God . . . gives me the freedom to acknowledge
my negative attitudes . . . but not the freedom
to act them out because they are as destructive
for me as they are for the other person.

Rebecca Manley Pippert

# When I'm overwhelmed by the cares of motherhood . . .

*Cast all your anxieties on him, for he cares about you.*
1 PETER 5:7 RSV

*Worry is a heavy load,*
*but a kind word cheers you up.*
PROVERBS 12:25 NCV

*Cast your burden upon the LORD and He will sustain you.*
PSALM 55:22 NASB

*[Jesus said] Take heed to yourselves, lest your hearts*
*be weighed down with carousing, drunkenness,*
*and cares of this life.*
LUKE 21:34 NKJV

*Jesus said, "Come to me, all of you who are weary and carry*
*heavy burdens, and I will give you rest. Take my yoke upon*
*you . . . and you will find rest for your souls. For my yoke fits*
*perfectly, and the burden I give you is light."*
MATTHEW 11:28-30 NLT

# . . . I will pray.

Father God,

When my child came into this world, I felt nothing but bliss and thankfulness over becoming a mother. After a while, though, the intense responsibility began to weigh on me. I'm always on guard, ready to run to my child when he cries.

At times I can help solve my child's problems or soothe a scraped knee. But, Lord, I need Your help when the troubles loom too large. Only You can heal the wounded knee—or a wounded spirit. Whatever the size of the challenge, Lord, You are bigger. Nothing is too difficult for You.

Father, when I am troubled, I call on You. You answer in Your time and according to Your plan, and just as I comfort my child, You comfort me. Help me overcome obstacles. Renew me and give me strength and peace.

I bring my cares to You because I know You care for me. Help me to remember the bliss I felt in those first few days of motherhood, and help me to lay my worries down. They're too heavy for me to carry anyway.

You are always on guard, ready to hear me when I cry, and I thank You.

Amen.

Man's world has become a nervous one, encompassed by anxiety. God's world is other than this; always balanced, calm, and in order.

Faith Baldwin

# When I'm dealing with change in my relationship with my child . . .

[Moses said] The LORD himself will go before you.
He will be with you; he will not leave you or forget you.
Don't be afraid and don't worry.

DEUTERONOMY 31:8 NCV

[God said] I'll go ahead of you, clearing and paving the road.

ISAIAH 45:2 MSG

[The Lord says] Do not remember the former things,
Nor consider the things of old. Behold, I will do a new thing,
Now it shall spring forth; Shall you not know it?
I will even make a road in the wilderness
and rivers in the desert.

ISAIAH 43:18-19 NKJV

✿

I am the Lord, I change not.

MALACHI 3:6 KJV

# . . . I will pray.

Heavenly Father,

Today when my child came in from school, I did a double take. Where did this teenager who ran in my front door come from, and what did she do with my little girl? These days it seems I'm left in the dust as she moves full speed ahead.

Sometimes I long for the sweet doll baby who crawled up into my lap and let me stroke her hair so I could tell her stories and snuggle with her. Now I'm blessed if I get more than three or four words out of this youngster as she flies by me to answer the phone—talking to friends is much more interesting than talking to Mom.

I've raised her the best I can; now please help me to accept this different relationship with my child. As she becomes more independent, I know I need to accept the changes that are bound to happen. Help me to relinquish her into Your hands and into Your care.

Even though she doesn't seem to need me, just as You're always waiting to love me, I'll always be there for her to show her my love.

Amen.

❖

Every end is a new beginning.
Robert Harold Schuller

# When my children don't understand me . . .

*I gain understanding from your precepts;*
*therefore I hate every wrong path.*
PSALM 119:104

✿

*The fear of the LORD is the beginning of wisdom;*
*a good understanding have all those who practice it.*
PSALM 111:10 RSV

✿

*[David said] The LORD knows what is in everyone's mind.*
*He understands everything you think. If you go*
*to him for help, you will get an answer.*
1 CHRONICLES 28:9 NCV

✿

*Help me understand, so I can keep your teachings.*
PSALM 119:34 NCV

✿

*Your rules are always good.*
*Help me understand so I can live.*
PSALM 119:144 NCV

# . . . I will pray.

Lord God,

Before I became a mother, I studied all the material I could get my hands on in hopes of becoming the perfect mom. I still strive to be the best I can be for my children. Sometimes I have to make decisions and do things my children just don't understand, and do they ever complain!

As I was growing up, there were times I didn't understand the decisions my parents made either. I realize now, however, that although they weren't perfect, they acted out of love for me. Now the shoe rests on the other foot. As a mother doing what I think is best, I have to be strong in my convictions. When my children don't understand, I pray that they will at least know that I have their best interests at heart. Lord, help my words and actions reflect the deep love I have for them.

I'm thankful that when it seems as if no one really understands me, I can kneel to pray and feel Your love fill my heart. You know the deepest, darkest parts of me, and yet You still love and understand me. Let me love and teach my family and lead them to You.

Amen.

It's taken me all my life to understand that
it is not necessary to understand everything.

René-Jules-Gustave Coty

# When I'm in conflict with my child . . .

*Pursue peace with all people.*
HEBREWS 12:14 NKJV

*Whoever is slow to anger has great understanding,*
*but one who has a hasty temper exalts folly.*
PROVERBS 14:29 NRSV

*A soft answer turns away wrath,*
*but a harsh word stirs up anger.*
PROVERBS 15:1 NRSV

*Those who are hot-tempered stir up strife,*
*but those who are slow to anger calm contention.*
PROVERBS 15:18 NRSV

*A fool gives full vent to anger,*
*but the wise quietly holds it back.*
PROVERBS 29:11 NRSV

# . . . I will pray.

O Lord,

Not long ago I had a home filled with peace and contentment. Now every day I seem to be in conflict with my child over something. Sometimes we fuss over big issues, but more often, trivial things cause continuing battles—like two porcupines in a sack, rubbing each other the wrong way, sticking each other at every turn.

Lord, I know You are a God of peace. I ask that You bring peace into our hearts and back into our relationship. Help me contain my anger so I won't overreact and lose control. I ask for wisdom to see the source of our conflict in a detached way so I can be fair.

I love my child so much, and I don't want to fight to win or prove this young one wrong. In the midst of a heated argument, guard my mouth so I won't say things I'll regret later.

It would be wonderful to have a peaceful relationship once more. Lord, I know that may be something I have to wait for, so grant me patience. I look to You, Lord, for my help.

Amen.

To handle yourself, use your head.
To handle others, use your heart.

Donald Laird

# When I need courage to do the right thing for my child . . .

*Those who spare the rod hate their children,*
*but those who love them are diligent to discipline them.*
PROVERBS 13:24 NRSV

✿

*Discipline your children while there is hope;*
*do not set your heart on their destruction.*
PROVERBS 19:18 NRSV

✿

*A youngster's heart is filled with foolishness,*
*but discipline will drive it away.*
PROVERBS 22:15 NLT

✿

*Discipline your children, and they will give you rest;*
*they will give delight to your heart.*
PROVERBS 29:17 NRSV

✿

*Do not exasperate your children; instead,*
*bring them up in the training and instruction of the Lord.*
EPHESIANS 6:4

# . . . I will pray.

Father God,

I need courage. My child's behavior has gotten out of control, and once again I must discipline him. I admit, being a disciplinarian is my least-favorite task as a mother. It would be much easier to let things slide, but then I would not be fulfilling my responsibility to train my child in Your ways.

I know it's the right and appropriate step for me to take, and so I ask for courage and godly wisdom. Sometimes my child resents me for doing the right thing. Lord, work through me as I raise him. Help me to make choices that will glorify You.

I ask that You refine my child's character through all this. Give him strength and courage to face peer pressure. Lead him to godly relationships and deliver him from those who would steer him wrong. You can use this bad situation and turn it into something that brings You glory. The prospect of a joyous outcome gives me hope in the midst of this trial.

And, Lord, please give my child a special understanding of a mother's love. Restore our relationship with one another in Your time.

Amen.

Our tendency is to grab and hold our children and not allow them to make mistakes. Then, when they do fail, we jump forward to bail them out and prevent them from learning valuable lessons.

James C. Dobson

# When I'm struggling with depression . . .

*He will not break the bruised reed, nor quench the dimly*
*burning flame. He will encourage the fainthearted,*
*those tempted to despair.*
ISAIAH 42:3 TLB

*Why are you downcast, O my soul?*
*Why so disturbed within me?*
*Put your hope in God.*
PSALM 42:5

*My soul is downcast within me.*
*Yet this I call to mind*
*and therefore I have hope:*
*Because of the LORD'S great love we are not consumed,*
*for his compassions never fail.*
*They are new every morning;*
*great is your faithfulness.*
LAMENTATIONS 3:20-23

*Where does my help come from?*
*My help comes from the LORD,*
*the Maker of heaven and earth.*
PSALM 121:1-2

# . . . I will pray.

Lord God,

Lately I've had such a downcast view of life. Some days I don't even want to get out of bed. For some reason, the bad days have stretched into bad weeks. Lord, I come to You to share my deepest hurts, disappointments, and needs. The cares of this life threaten to overwhelm me, and I need You now.

When I'm in the middle of a valley, hoping for a ray of sunlight to shine into my world, I call on You. I have faith that Your strong arm will lift me out of my despair.

When my children have had a bad day, I comfort them by wiping away their tears, stroking the soft hair on their heads. When I pray, Lord, it's almost as if You stroke my hair as You comfort me. I wipe away my tears, and I'm assured that You will sustain me; and I know even though I may not see it today, one day I will see the sunshine.

Help me as I allow this depression to be the catalyst that drives me deeper into Your presence to find nourishment for my hungry soul.

Amen.

We ought to praise God even when we do not
feel like it. Praising him takes away the blues and
restores us to normal.

Harold Lindsell

# When my child is a disappointment to me . . .

*If you love someone you will be loyal to him no matter what the cost. You will always believe in him, always expect the best of him, and always stand your ground in defending him.*
1 CORINTHIANS 13:7 TLB

*Walk in love, as Christ loved us.*
EPHESIANS 5:2 RSV

*Above all, keep fervent in your love for one another, because love covers a multitude of sins.*
1 PETER 4:8 NASB

*Hatred stirs up strife,*
*But love covers all sins.*
PROVERBS 10:12 NKJV

*The rod of correction imparts wisdom,*
*but a child left to himself disgraces his mother.*
PROVERBS 29:15

# . . . I will pray.

Dear Lord,

My child has really disappointed me today. God, when You created us, You gave us a free will. And does my child ever exhibit a strong one! I need Your help as I cope with this child when he makes decisions I don't agree with or chooses a path I don't approve of.

When I began this journey through motherhood, I had such high expectations for both my child and myself. Perhaps those expectations have been unrealistic, setting me up for disappointment. If so, give me a more objective view. Show me how to set high standards that are more realistic.

My child is a lot like I am—far from perfect. Forgive me, Father, for the mistakes I've made. I'm humbled by the fact that You love me in spite of my shortcomings. Lord, help me to have this same attitude when my child is a disappointment to me. I turn my heart to You, God. You can give this imperfect soul perfect peace and guidance.

No matter what this child does, I continue to love without restraint. I pray for Your wisdom to guide him and ask that he will choose to live a life dedicated to You.

Amen.

Ideal parenting is modeled after the relationship between God and man.

James C. Dobson

# When I'm feeling discontent in my role as a mother . . .

*I have learned to be content in whatever circumstances I am.*
PHILIPPIANS 4:11 NASB

✿

*Godliness with contentment is great gain.*
1 TIMOTHY 6:6

✿

*Your wife shall be contented in your home. And look at
all those children! There they sit around the dinner table
as vigorous and healthy as young olive trees. That is
God's reward to those who reverence and trust him.*
PSALM 128:3-4 TLB

✿

*[Jesus said] You're blessed when you're content with just
who you are—no more, no less. That's the moment you find
yourselves proud owners of everything that can't be bought.*
MATTHEW 5:5 MSG

✿

*[Jesus said] If you're content to simply be yourself,
your life will count for plenty.*
MATTHEW 23:12 MSG

# . . . I will pray.

Lord God,

You know that on most days I'm thrilled and consider myself blessed beyond all measure to be a mom. I'm deeply grateful and humbled that You trust me with this most important job. I strive each day to instill godly values into my children—a real challenge in a world filled with sin and turmoil.

Sometimes, though, I have this nagging feeling that I don't even like to acknowledge—an underlying current of discontentment. Perhaps it's because with many jobs, I could mark off a checklist of my accomplishments at the end of each day. Not so in my role as a mother. There's no such thing as a quarterly job evaluation, nothing in black and white giving me feedback on how I'm doing, even though my performance affects others in such a profound way.

Lord, I trust You to help me to be content. Remind me often that even though I may not see progress daily, this job yields eternal benefits. My greatest desire is to see my children grow to love and serve You. Help me to be joyful in my role as a mother. Thank You, Father.

Amen.

Countless times each day a mother does what no one else can do quite as well. She wipes away a tear, whispers a word of hope, eases a child's fear. She teaches, ministers, loves, and nurtures the next generation of citizens. And she challenges and cajoles her kids to do their best and be the best.

James C. Dobson and Gary L. Bauer

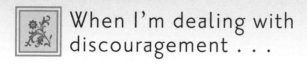

# When I'm dealing with discouragement . . .

*When I pray, you answer me;*
*you encourage me by giving me the strength I need.*
PSALM 138:3 NLT

*Let all who are discouraged take heart.*
*Let us praise the Lord together, and exalt his name.*
PSALM 34:2-3 TLB

*O my soul, don't be discouraged. Don't be upset.*
*Expect God to act! For I know that I shall again have plenty*
*of reason to praise him for all that he will do.*
*He is my help! He is my God!*
PSALM 42:11 TLB

*Be encouraged, you who worship God.*
*The LORD listens to those in need.*
PSALM 69:32-33 NCV

# . . . I will pray.

Heavenly Father,

It seems like not too long ago I could eat a meal without stopping to pick pieces of food off the floor. Menus didn't become paper airplanes, and other diners didn't stare at me as if they wished I would leave.

When the world spins faster and more out of control around me, I ask for emotional and spiritual strength. At times, the demands of motherhood fatigue me, and during the most stressful days, I feel like a failure. Much of my daily routine seems mundane: make breakfast, do laundry, clean, help with homework. Every day, I help my children in many ways.

I ask You for peace to soothe my soul. Fill my heart with encouragement, and when I'm weary, strengthen me. Lord, during this time of discouragement, please make Yourself real to me. You promise to be with me even when life gets wearisome, and I thank You that I can count on Your presence to calm me. When little things threaten to discourage me, help me see the big picture: my goal to raise godly children.

Thank You for being my Source of encouragement and hope.

Amen.

Should we feel at times disheartened and discouraged, a confiding thought, a simple movement of heart toward God will renew our powers. Whatever he may demand of us, he will give us at the moment the strength and the courage that we need.

François Fénelon

# When I need endurance . . .

*The one who endures to the end will be saved.*
MATTHEW 10:22 NRSV

*[Jesus said] In the good soil, these are the ones who, when they hear the word, hold it fast in an honest and good heart, and bear fruit with patient endurance.*
LUKE 8:15 NRSV

*When we see that you're just as willing to endure the hard times as to enjoy the good times, we know you're going to make it, no doubt about it.*
2 CORINTHIANS 1:7 MSG

*We pray that you'll have the strength to stick it out over the long haul—not the grim strength of gritting your teeth but the glory-strength God gives. It is strength that endures the unendurable and spills over into joy, thanking the Father who makes us strong enough to take part in everything bright and beautiful that he has for us.*
COLOSSIANS 1:11-12 MSG

# . . . I will pray.

Heavenly Father,

The first blush of motherhood has faded. Sometimes the path from infancy to adulthood looks endless. Amid the hustle and bustle of daily life, I find it easy to lose sight of my goal: raising my children to be godly people. What an incredibly demanding task!

Then I overheard my children as they played one day. My daughter imitated her mommy—even mimicking my way of speaking. I secretly watched as she patted her little brother on the head and gave him his plate of pretend food. Thank You for allowing me to witness that scene. It reminded me that little eyes watch my every step. Lord, help me to be the best mommy I can be and to model Your attributes before my children. God, I pray my words and actions represent those of a godly mother.

I will persevere. It's not in my nature to give up when life gets tough. Older moms have told me my children will be grown before I know it. Although that seems unbelievable right now, I trust You for endurance as I travel this road with Your help and strength.

Amen.

Nothing great was ever done without much enduring.

Catherine of Siena

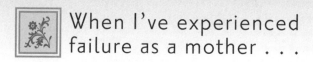# When I've experienced failure as a mother . . .

*The LORD has heard my cry for mercy;*
*the LORD accepts my prayer.*
PSALM 6:9

*O God, you have declared me perfect in your eyes; you have*
*always cared for me in my distress; now hear me as I call*
*again. Have mercy on me. Hear my prayer.*
PSALM 4:1 TLB

*I am radiant with joy because of your mercy,*
*for you have listened to my troubles*
*and have seen the crisis in my soul.*
PSALM 31:7 TLB

✿

*Listen to my cries for mercy.*
*If you, God, kept records on wrongdoings,*
*who would stand a chance?*
*As it turns out, forgiveness is your habit,*
*and that's why you're worshiped.*
PSALM 130:2-4 MSG

# . . . I will pray.

Dear Lord,

It happened again. I told myself it wouldn't, but it did. I feel like such a failure, as if I will never be the kind of mother my children deserve. Why can't I get it right? Why do my children have to suffer for my shortcomings?

I know in my heart that no one is flawless. So why do I strive for perfection and beat myself up when I fall short?

I wonder how You see my failure. Do You roll Your eyes and shake Your head at my sin? No, of course not. You scoop me up in Your heavenly embrace and hold me until I feel the warmth of Your forgiveness.

Lord, encourage my soul and help me overcome the doubts and self-criticism that have crept into my life. My failure as a parent is draining me of energy. Recharge me with Your divine strength and help me to see myself as You see me: not as a failure but as Your child who sometimes stumbles over bumps in the road of growth. And forgive me for veering off the trail and failing to travel the path You have already paved for me.

Amen.

A failure is not someone who has tried and failed;
it is someone who has given up trying and
resigned himself to failure;
it is not a condition, but an attitude.

Sydney J. Harris

# When I need faith for
my child . . .

*Do not cast away your confidence, which has great reward.*

*May you be able to feel and understand, as all God's children
should, how long, how wide, how deep, and how high his love
really is; and to experience this love for yourselves, though it
is so great that you will never see the end of it or fully know
or understand it. And so at last you will be
filled up with God himself.*
EPHESIANS 3:18-19 TLB

*I do not cease to give thanks for you, remembering you
in my prayers, that the God of our Lord Jesus Christ, the
Father of glory, may give you a spirit of wisdom and of
revelation in the knowledge of him, having the eyes
of your hearts enlightened, that you may know
what is the hope to which he has called you.*
EPHESIANS 1:16-18 RSV

*[ Jesus, quoting the father of the prodigal son, said]
This son of mine was dead and has now returned to life.
He was lost, but now he is found.*
LUKE 15:24 NLT

# . . . I will pray.

Renewer of Faith,

Sometimes I wonder if my child will ever grow and mature into a productive adult whose heart is devoted to You. She struggles in so many areas of her life. Her spirit seems restless, and she is always searching, struggling to find that one thing that will make her happy. Will she ever grab hold of Your Word and let it sink deep into her soul?

My faith wanes as we battle in the same arena day after day. The situation seems hopeless. I know my constant nagging and discouragement only make her attitude worse.

God, I need You to encourage me and give me Your eyes, so I may see her as You do. Magnify her positive qualities and show me little ways I can build her up and encourage her heart.

When my faith is weak, strengthen my spirit by the promises You have made to me in Your Word. Draw my child close to me and create a bond in us, strengthened by You, that can never be broken. Thank You for renewing my faith for my child.

Amen.

Faith can put a candle in the darkest night.

Margaret Sangster

# When I'm dealing with fear regarding my child . . .

Do not be afraid of sudden panic,
or of the storm that strikes the wicked;
for the LORD will be your confidence
and will keep your foot from being caught.
PROVERBS 3:25-26 NRSV

I am holding you by your right hand—
I, the LORD your God. And I say to you,
"Do not be afraid. I am here to help you."
ISAIAH 41:13 NLT

You will not fear the terror of the night,
nor the arrow that flies by day,
nor the pestilence that stalks in darkness,
nor the destruction that wastes at noonday.
A thousand may fall at your side,
ten thousand at your right hand;
but it will not come near you.
PSALM 91:5-7 RSV

The angel of the LORD encamps around those who fear Him,
And rescues them.
PSALM 34:7 NASB

# . . . I will pray.

God of Peace,

Fear is trying to cover me like a dark cloud. Anxiety over-casts my sunny disposition and I am afraid for my children, their safety, their futures, their lives. Though my rational mind tells me I shouldn't be afraid, my insides churn with the knowl-edge of all the things that could happen to them.

I try to shut out the thunder of worry, but sometimes the fear is too powerful. I know when I dwell on it, the terror grows like a gathering storm and takes on a life of its own. When I let go of my worries, despite how I'm feeling, that is when I find Your rest for my troubled soul.

The storms of life have caused me to fear and fret. Lord, help me to exchange these negative emotions for Your peace now. Hold me in Your love and reassurance to help me over-come my anxiety regarding my children. Let Your presence light up the darkness that has fallen over my heart and clouded my mind. Let Your peace fall down on me like a gentle rain. Thank You for calming the storm.

Amen.

God incarnate is the end of fear;
and the heart that realizes
that he is in the midst . . .
will be quiet in the midst of alarm.

F. B. Meyer

# When my child is experiencing a problem with finances . . .

*I have been young, and now am old; yet have I not seen the righteous forsaken, nor his seed begging bread.*
PSALM 37:25 KJV

*This same God who takes care of me will supply all your needs from his glorious riches, which have been given to us in Christ Jesus.*
PHILIPPIANS 4:19 NLT

*Money that comes easily disappears quickly, but money that is gathered little by little will grow.*
PROVERBS 13:11 NCV

*The earnings of the godly enhance their lives.*
PROVERBS 10:16 NLT

❀

*Pay all your debts except the debt of love for others —never finish paying that!*
ROMANS 13:8 TLB

# . . . I will pray.

Providing Lord,

My son is having financial difficulties and I feel it might be my fault. Did I give him too much when he was little? I had so little growing up, and I wanted only to give him everything I didn't have: the best designer clothes, the latest tennis shoes, tennis lessons. Maybe I shouldn't have handed everything to him so readily. When he had a need, all he had to do was ask Mom and I'd fill his wallet. I should have shown him how to be more responsible with his money. Now he's struggling, unable to manage his finances properly.

But I can't change the past; I can only alter the future. I can choose to bail him out of his current financial problems by handing him the money he needs, or I can support him through this crisis, offering some insights instead. I won't turn my back on my child during this time of need, but I don't want to continue to leave him unequipped for life.

Lord, give me the strength to do the right thing for my child, not the easy thing. Help him make good choices, and help me teach him to rely on You to meet all of his needs.

Amen.

Jesus talked a great deal about money
and the problems it causes man—in fact,
one-fifth of all Jesus had to say was about money.

Billy Graham

# When I need to forgive my child . . .

*Peter came to [Jesus] and asked, "Lord, how often should
I forgive someone who sins against me? Seven times?"
"No!" Jesus replied, "seventy times seven!"*
MATTHEW 18:21-22 NLT

✿

*[Love] is not rude (unmannerly) and does not act
unbecomingly. Love (God's love in us) does not insist on its
own rights or its own way, for it is not self-seeking; it is not
touchy or fretful or resentful; it takes no account of the evil
done to it [it pays no attention to a suffered wrong].
It does not rejoice at injustice and unrighteousness,
but rejoices when right and truth prevail.*
1 CORINTHIANS 13:5-6 AMP

✿

*[Jesus said] Judge not, and you will not be judged;
condemn not, and you will not be condemned;
forgive, and you will be forgiven.*
LUKE 6:37 RSV

✿

*Jesus said, "Father, forgive them; for
they know not what they do."*
LUKE 23:34 RSV

# . . . I will pray.

Forgiving Lord,

Sometimes when my child tests me, I am able to forgive and move on. But other times he pushes me beyond what I can bear. I often wonder if being a parent is worth all the struggles, the disappointment, the pain and failure.

I know deep inside that no matter how old my child becomes, he's still learning and growing, just as I am. But sometimes it's so hard to forgive those things he continues to do over and over again. How many times must I forgive?

But then I hear Your voice echo in my ears.

"Seventy times seven."

How many times do I want You to forgive me? Every time I fail, of course. So why should I offer less to my child?

Lord, fill my heart with grace and mercy for my child. Stir up compassion in my soul when he offends me. Help me to see him through Your eyes, that I will always love him and, yes, forgive him—just as You will always forgive me. Thank You for Your unconditional grace.

Amen.

Humanity is never so beautiful as when praying for forgiveness or else forgiving another.

Jean Paul Richter

# When I need help understanding God's will for my child . . .

*[Not in your own strength] for it is God Who is all the while effectually at work in you [energizing and creating in you the power and desire], both to will and to work for His good pleasure and satisfaction and delight.*

PHILIPPIANS 2:13 AMP

✿

*As your plan unfolds, even the simple can understand it.*

PSALM 119:130 TLB

✿

*David said, "All these plans were written with the LORD guiding me. He helped me understand everything in the plans."*

1 CHRONICLES 28:19 NCV

✿

*"I know what I am planning for you," says the LORD. "I have good plans for you, not plans to hurt you. I will give you hope and a good future."*

JEREMIAH 29:11 NCV

✿

*[Jesus said] Anyone who does God's will is my brother, and my sister, and my mother.*

MARK 3:35 TLB

# . . . I will pray.

All-Knowing Father,

From the moment my children were born, I could see differences in them. One arrived ahead of schedule, the other a few days late. As toddlers their differences showed through the way they played. One is a go-getter, whereas the other is more laid-back. I've often wondered how two opposite children could come from the same parents.

Now that they're older, I see those things they enjoyed as children blossoming into gifts and talents given by You. Their interests, hobbies, and personalities have a purpose. It's Your way of giving me a glimpse into their futures—their destinies. Yet, I get concerned. Am I steering them in the right direction for their lives?

Lord, I believe You've had a plan for my children from the beginning of time and that You have a specific purpose for each one. Reveal to me Your will for their lives, and give me wisdom and restraint if I stray off the trail You have chosen. Speak to their spirits and guide their every step. Thank You for being the Gift-Giver and Director of our lives.

Amen.

The whole science of the saints consists in finding out
and following God's will.

Isidore of Seville

# When I need help explaining God's Word to my child . . .

*Your word is a lamp to my feet
and a light for my path.*
PSALM 119:105

*Hear my cry to you, LORD.
Let your word help me understand.*
PSALM 119:169 NCV

*If you want better insight and discernment, and are searching
for them as you would for lost money or hidden treasure, then
wisdom will be given you, and knowledge of God himself; you
will soon learn the importance of reverence for the Lord and
of trusting him. For the Lord grants wisdom! His every word
is a treasure of knowledge and understanding.*
PROVERBS 2:3-6 TLB

*Lead me in Your truth and teach me.*
PSALM 25:5 NASB

# . . . I will pray.

Father of Light,

My child asked me a question about Your Word and I didn't have an answer again. I held my breath, hoping he wouldn't ask me to explain what I had just read, but he did.

I glossed over the question and directed his focus to something I did understand. But what happens when that question arises again? Or another one that I can't answer? I don't want to put him off, especially when he's so eager to learn about You. But how can I explain something I don't fully grasp myself?

Lord, quiet my mind and help me see through the eyes of a child. Speak to my soul and reveal the things You want me to share from Your Word. Help me not to doubt myself but instead to hear Your voice and be confident that You have spoken to my heart. Reveal to me the things my child will understand and put the words into my mouth, so I don't cause him to stumble as he grows closer to You. Thank You for shining light on Your Word.

Amen.

Come, Holy Ghost, for moved by thee
The prophets wrote and spoke;
Unlock the truth, thyself the key,
Unseal the sacred book.

John Calvin

# When I need guidance in regard to my child . . .

*Train children in the right way,*
*and when old, they will not stray.*
PROVERBS 22:6 NRSV

*In your unfailing love you will lead*
*the people you have redeemed.*
*In your strength you will guide them*
*to your holy dwelling.*
EXODUS 15:13

*He guides me in paths of righteousness*
*for his name's sake.*
PSALM 23:3

*He guides the humble in what is right*
*and teaches them his way.*
PSALM 25:9

*I will teach you wisdom's ways and lead you in*
*straight paths. If you live a life guided by wisdom,*
*you won't limp or stumble as you run.*
PROVERBS 4:11-12 NLT

# . . . I will pray.

Dear Lord,

I look at my child and wonder, *Will she ever fit into society's mold?* She struggles in certain areas of life and excels in others. Yet, so many times she's the odd one out, the underdog, fighting against all odds to be king of the hill.

We've tried to encourage her in the areas she excels in and direct her down the roads that will lead to success. We've shielded her from potential social difficulties and pain. But is that the best thing for her? Maybe it's time we push her out of the nest.

Lord, how did You let go of Your Son when You knew what His future was? It had to have been painful. But You still did it.

God, give me guidance as I prepare my child for the turbulence of life. Though the skies she travels may not be clear, help me to equip her and guide her with what she needs to arrive at her destination unscathed. Show me when she should leave the shelter of my wings. May she soar like an eagle when that time comes.

Amen.

God is an ever-present Spirit guiding all that happens to a wise and holy end.

David Hume

# When I need to provide a stable home for my child . . .

*It takes wisdom to have a good family,*
*and it takes understanding to make it strong.*
*It takes knowledge to fill a home*
*with rare and beautiful treasures.*
PROVERBS 24:3-4 NCV

*The work of righteousness will be peace,*
*And the effect of righteousness, quietness and assurance*
*forever. My people will dwell in a peaceful habitation,*
*In secure dwellings, and in quiet resting places.*
ISAIAH 32:17-18 NKJV

*[The Lord] will be the stability of your times.*
ISAIAH 33:6 NASB

*Life rooted in God stands firm.*
PROVERBS 12:3 MSG

*Unless the LORD builds the house,*
*They labor in vain who build it;*
*Unless the LORD guards the city,*
*The watchman keeps awake in vain.*
PSALM 127:1 NASB

# . . . I will pray.

Unwavering Lord,

Life has gotten crazy lately. My marriage is strained, the bills from last month still need to be paid, and the chaos in our home has escalated to Dr. Phil levels. The kids are overcommitted with school and extracurricular activities. I'm exhausted from carting them from place to place. We're all tired and irritable. Their unruly conduct, especially in public, is out of control. But I know their behavior just mimics the stress we're living with. How can I bring peace to this unstable home?

I admit, we've neglected our time with You. I've put You off many times while trying to douse the fires that burn out of control all around me. We've forgotten our family commitment to each other—those fun times when we simply enjoy staying home and being together. My husband and I have neglected each other as well.

God, thank You for never changing—for being there when our home starts to buckle under the pressure. Quench the anxiety in my spirit. Change me. Change my heart so I may be an example for my family to follow. Thank You for the quiet embers of Your Spirit, which burn only to light our path.

Amen.

Anyone can build a house:
we need the Lord for the creation of a home.

John Henry Jowett

When I need hope . . .

O LORD my God, I cried to you for help,
and you have healed me.
O LORD, you brought up my soul from Sheol,
restored me to life from among those gone down to the Pit.
PSALM 30:2-3 NRSV

I said, "What good will it do if I die
or if I go down to the grave?
Dust cannot praise you;
it cannot speak about your truth.
LORD, hear me and have mercy on me.
LORD, help me."
You changed my sorrow into dancing.
You took away my clothes of sadness,
and clothed me in happiness.
I will sing to you and not be silent.
LORD, my God, I will praise you forever.
PSALM 30:9-12 NCV

✿

I am still confident of this:
I will see the goodness of the LORD
in the land of the living.
Wait for the LORD;
be strong and take heart
and wait for the LORD.
PSALM 27:13-14 NIV

# . . . I will pray.

Sustaining Lord,

Every time I think things will change for the better with my child, the walls of reality come crumbling down around me and I am buried deeper in despair than I had been before.

I can't see the light.

My situation seems hopeless.

No matter how hard I try to dig myself out, I seem to slide back down into my hole. Even if I burrow out from it, will there be anything worth salvaging?

I am weary from the constant battle I wage as a mom. I need You to pull me out of this pit I have gotten myself into. Only You can save me and restore my hope. Only You can strengthen me and give me the will to continue in this journey of parenting. Set me on firm ground and dust me off so I am able to move ahead.

God, I'm reaching up through the hopelessness. Grab hold of my hands and don't let go. Pull me out of the muck and mire into Your glorious light. Your loving light. Your hopeful light. Thank You for restoring my strength and peace. I will hope in You.

Amen.

God be praised, that to believing souls
Gives light in darkness, comfort in despair!

William Shakespeare

# When I've suffered the loss of a child . . .

*My soul weeps because of grief;*
*Strengthen me according to Your word.*
PSALM 119:28 NASB

*Surely He has borne our griefs*
*And carried our sorrows.*
ISAIAH 53:4 NKJV

*I cry to you, O LORD;*
*I say, "You are my refuge,*
*my portion in the land of the living."*
*Listen to my cry,*
*for I am in desperate need;*
*rescue me from those who pursue me,*
*for they are too strong for me.*
*Set me free from my prison,*
*that I may praise your name.*
PSALM 142:5-7

*All praise to the God and Father of our Lord Jesus Christ.*
*He is the source of every mercy and the God who*
*comforts us. He comforts us in all our troubles*
*so that we can comfort others.*
2 CORINTHIANS 1:3-4 NLT

# . . . I will pray.

Comforting Father,

It makes no sense. She was so beautiful, so full of life and love. My arms ache to hold her once more. My heart cries out from the gaping hole left behind by her death. The wound is so fresh and deep. No one knows how I feel. They just don't understand my pain.

God, You are a father. You watched Your Child die, but You knew His death held a greater purpose. Though I can't see the reason for my child's death, I won't try to make sense of it. Instead, I choose to celebrate her life. When I remember her, I feel only joy.

Lord, comfort me. You know what it feels like to suffer the death of a child. You alone can heal my pain. I know my child is safe in Your arms. Hold her tight and tell her I miss her. Fill in the wound of my heart with the memories of my daughter, her bright smile and tender spirit. The scar on my heart will always remain, but I know I can be whole again. Thank You for healing my heart.

Amen.

On the wings of time grief flies away.

Jean de La Fontaine

# When I need a miracle for my child . . .

*Remember the world of wonders he has made, his miracles,*
*. . . He's GOD, our God, in charge of the whole earth.*
*And he remembers, remembers his Covenant—*
*for a thousand generations he's been as good as his word.*
PSALM 105:5,7-8 MSG

*O Lord my God, many and many a time you have done great*
*miracles for us, and we are ever in your thoughts. Who else*
*can do such glorious things?*
PSALM 40:5 TLB

*How we thank you, Lord!*
*Your mighty miracles give proof that you care.*
PSALM 75:1 TLB

✿

*Answer my prayers, O LORD,*
*for your unfailing love is wonderful.*
*Turn and take care of me,*
*for your mercy is so plentiful.*
PSALM 69:16 NLT

# . . . I will pray.

Tender Lord,

My heart aches at the thought of my child hurting. Though he may put on a brave face, I know he suffers inside. As his mom, I wish I could do something to ease his pain and lighten his anxiety.

I would change places with him if I could.

But I can't.

I know You don't want to see him in this situation. Like any good parent, You desire health, happiness, and prosperity for him. So You know why I'm praying for this miracle in my child's life. You know the pain parents go through when their child suffers. Take away that pain by giving my son the miracle—the breakthrough—he so desperately needs.

Father, I believe You want my child to be happy. Heal his body, mind, and spirit. Sustain him as You bring him through this trial; and when he emerges on the other side, make him stronger and happier than he was before. Thank You, Lord, for hearing this mother's cry, for rushing to the side of my child and for making him whole.

Amen.

A miracle is an event beyond the power
of any known physical law to produce;
it is a spiritual occurrence produced by
the power of God, a marvel, a wonder.

Billy Graham

# When I need patience . . .

*Love is patient and kind.*
1 CORINTHIANS 13:4 RSV

*Be patient with each person, attentive to individual needs.
And be careful that when you get on each other's nerves
you don't snap at each other.*
1 THESSALONIANS 5:14-15 MSG

*Be humble and gentle. Be patient with each other, making
allowance for each other's faults because of your love.
Always keep yourselves united in the Holy Spirit, and
bind yourselves together with peace.*
EPHESIANS 4:2-3 NLT

*As God's chosen people, holy and dearly loved,
clothe yourselves with compassion, kindness, humility,
gentleness and patience.*
COLOSSIANS 3:12

*The Lord's servant must not be quarrelsome but
kindly to everyone, . . . patient.*
2 TIMOTHY 2:24 NRSV

# . . . I will pray.

Lord God,

I tell my children to have patience when they're waiting for their lunch or when sharing a toy, but I feel like such a hypocrite. I just lost my patience with them! How can I expect them to behave when I can't set a good example for them to follow?

Lord, I confess I'm impatient not only with my children, but with others as well. I complain when I'm waiting in line at the grocery store or when I'm stuck in traffic. My soul is always anxious. I'm constantly uptight about the next thing and unable to enjoy the moment.

God, forgive me. I really have no right to lose my patience when You've been so patient with me. You've never tired of waiting for me, and You're always there when I finally decide to show up. Lord, forgive me for my childish behavior, my irritation with my children and others. Help me walk in Your peace so I can enjoy the moment, so I don't simply hurry on to the next thing. Silence the voice of impatience that plays in my head and replace it with Your love.

Amen.

Patience is the companion of wisdom.

Saint Augustine of Hippo

# When I need peace . . .

*What happens when we live God's way?*
*He brings gifts into our lives, much the same way that fruit*
*appears in an orchard—things like . . . serenity.*
<small>GALATIANS 5:22 MSG</small>

*[God said]*
*Blessed is the man who trusts me, GOD,*
*the woman who sticks with GOD.*
*They're like trees replanted in Eden,*
*putting down roots near the rivers—*
*Never a worry through the hottest of summers,*
*never dropping a leaf,*
*Serene and calm through droughts,*
*bearing fresh fruit every season.*
<small>JEREMIAH 17:7-8 MSG</small>

*A tranquil mind gives life to the flesh.*
<small>PROVERBS 14:30 NRSV</small>

*[Jesus said] I am leaving you with a gift—peace of mind and*
*heart. And the peace I give isn't like the peace the world*
*gives. So don't be troubled or afraid.*
<small>JOHN 14:27 NLT</small>

# . . . I will pray.

Calming God,

The stress of life is overwhelming me. I try to keep up with the demands, but I fall short of doing everything I feel I should as a mom. How do other moms do it and stay sane?

I remember a time when I felt Your peace, Your presence. It was before marriage, before kids, before I had any real responsibility. I made time to do the things that brought me tranquility.

I made time for You.

Just because this season of my life is more demanding, I know I still should be able to find serenity. Remind me that I don't have to let society drive my joy away by demanding my time and energy. I don't have to be a slave to my children or live up to the expectations that I place on myself.

Lord, help me to rest in Your presence, to slow down long enough to read Your Word, even if it is only for a few minutes each day. Thank You for being with me, even when I'm moving too fast to notice You. Thank You for offering Your peace and waiting for me to accept it.

Amen.

God is a tranquil being and abides in a tranquil eternity. So must your spirit become a tranquil and clear little pool, wherein the serene light of God can be mirrored.

Gerhard Tersteegen

# When I need help providing for my child . . .

*[Jesus said] Do not worry, saying, 'What shall we eat?'
or 'What shall we drink?' or 'What shall we wear?'
For the pagans run after all these things, and your heavenly
Father knows that you need them. But seek first
his kingdom and his righteousness, and all these things
will be given to you as well.*

MATTHEW 6:31-33

*He who supplies seed to the sower and bread for food
will supply and multiply your seed for sowing and increase
the harvest of your righteousness.*

2 CORINTHIANS 9:10 NRSV

*He satisfies the thirsty
and fills the hungry with good things.*

PSALM 107:9 NLT

*Good people have enough to eat,
but the wicked will go hungry.*

PROVERBS 13:25 NCV

# . . . I will pray.

Providing Lord,

I really need Your help right now. How are we going to make it? The stress of living paycheck to paycheck has worn me out. I hate worrying about such things as whether or not my children will have the medicine, food, and shelter they need to stay healthy. Then there are clothes, school supplies, and all the rest. I should be able to provide for them, but I'm having trouble doing that.

Should I swallow my pride and ask for help? If so, show me where I can find it. Is it Your will for me to go back to school so I can get a better-paying job? Whatever it takes, I'm willing to do it.

God, I trust You will provide for my family in the way You see best. Whether You drop the money into my lap or I have to get a different job, I know You will sustain me through this difficult time. When the unpaid bills pile up, I won't worry, for You will take care of us. You are my Provider, my Comforter in times of need. I will trust in You.

Amen.

The Lord my pasture shall prepare,
And feed me with a shepherd's care;
His presence shall my wants supply,
And guard me with a watchful eye.

Joseph Addison

# When I'm struggling with my past relationship with my child . . .

[Jesus said] Stop judging others, and you will not be judged.
For others will treat you as you treat them.

MATTHEW 7:1-2 NLT

[Jesus said] Here is a simple, rule-of-thumb guide for
behavior: Ask yourself what you want people to do for you,
then grab the initiative and do it for them.

MATTHEW 7:12 MSG

If someone does wrong to you,
do not pay him back by doing wrong to him.
Try to do what everyone thinks is right.
Do your best to live in peace with everyone.

ROMANS 12:17-18 NCV

✿

Avoid foolish controversies and . . . strife.

TITUS 3:9 NASB

# . . . I will pray.

Lord God,

My relationship with my child has been strained for so long. I could easily list all the ways that she's offended me and she could do the same. But what good would that do? What's done is done. It can never be changed—only forgiven.

Just as my relationship with You was restored, I know my bond with my child can be renewed. Help us see past the pain we've caused each other. I want to forget all the hurt and start over fresh. But it is so easy to slip back into those selfish behaviors that started the disharmony to begin with.

I know You are the God of second chances, so I'm asking You for one. Though we may not be able to forget the past, help us to forgive and move on. And if we offend each other again, we know we can forgive again. Help us to develop healthy, positive ways of relating to one another. Help us to be the support You have intended us to be to each other since the day she was born. Thank You for the precious gift of family.

Amen.

Wherever our life touches yours, we help or hinder . . .
wherever your life touches ours,
you make us stronger or weaker . . .
There is no escape—man drags man down,
or man lifts man up.

Booker T. Washington

# When I need rest . . .

*Return to your rest, O my soul,*
*For the LORD has dealt bountifully with you.*
*For You have rescued my soul from death,*
*My eyes from tears,*
*My feet from stumbling.*
PSALM 116:7-8 NASB

*[The Lord] lets me rest in green pastures.*
*He leads me to calm water.*
*He gives me new strength.*
PSALM 23:2-3 NCV

*I find rest in God; only he can save me.*
*. . . I find rest in God; only he gives me hope.*
PSALM 62:1,5 NCV

*Then Jesus said, "Come to me, all of you who are weary*
*and carry heavy burdens, and I will give you rest. Take my*
*yoke upon you. Let me teach you, because I am humble and*
*gentle, and you will find rest for your souls. For my yoke fits*
*perfectly, and the burden I give you is light."*
MATTHEW 11:28-30 NLT

# . . . I will pray.

Loving Lord,

I've finished my work for the evening, though there is much more I need to do. My body aches from an invisible load that weighs me down. I am worn-out, yet when I lay my head down to sleep, I am restless.

I need to get to bed earlier and slow down during the day, but how can I when the world around me seems to be spinning out of control? So many people are counting on me. How can I neglect my responsibilities, my work, my children?

My children.

They don't deserve an irritable, tired mother. They need a loving, compassionate mom. A rested mom.

Lord, quiet my soul in the midst of the chaos of life. Help me seek refuge under Your shelter. Though the whirlwind continues to blow around me, I am comforted in Your presence. In You I can find the rest I need, whether I am awake or asleep. Calm my body, my spirit, my soul so I can nurture those I love.

Thank You for providing a safe place where I can rest.

Amen.

There is no music in a rest,
but there is the making of music in it.

John Ruskin

# When I'm experiencing trials . . .

*[The Lord] reached down from heaven and*
*took me and drew me out of my great trials.*
*He rescued me from deep waters.*
PSALM 18:16 TLB

*Count it all joy when you fall into various trials,*
*knowing that the testing of your faith produces patience.*
*But let patience have its perfect work, that you may be perfect*
*and complete, lacking nothing.*
JAMES 1:2-4 NKJV

*Beloved, do not think it strange concerning the fiery trial*
*which is to try you, as though some strange thing happened to*
*you; but rejoice to the extent that you partake of Christ's*
*sufferings, that when His glory is revealed, you may also*
*be glad with exceeding joy.*
1 PETER 4:12-13 NKJV

*Anyone who meets a testing challenge head-on and manages*
*to stick it out is mighty fortunate. For such persons loyally in*
*love with God, the reward is life and more life.*
JAMES 1:12 MSG

# . . . I will pray.

Refining Father,

When I held my newborn in my arms for the first time, I couldn't imagine the trials that lay in store. First the exhaustion from sleepless nights, then the endless laundry, diapers, and feedings. The toddler years were trying, too, with temper tantrums and power struggles. Bouts of rebellion and strife have been a challenge ever since.

I have often wondered why my child and I clash so much, but I draw comfort from Your Word that says children are a reward and that You desire me to be a joyful mother. You give me joy in the midst of the challenges.

Trials are never fun, but I can see that each one I have faced has made me a better mother. Just as carbon becomes a diamond under pressure, these troubles of parenting have made me stronger.

Brighter.

More brilliant.

Even priceless.

Lord, comfort and strengthen me with Your presence when the pressures of parenting threaten to squeeze the life out of me. Help me to learn from each trial. Thank You for the ongoing transformation of my life, so I can shine brightly for You.

Amen.

We are always in the forge, or on the anvil;
by trials God is shaping us for higher things.
Henry Ward Beecher

# When I need wisdom to deal with my child . . .

*Wisdom puts light in the eyes,*
*And gives gentleness to words and manners.*
ECCLESIASTES 8:1 MSG

*A good person speaks with wisdom,*
*and he says what is fair.*
PSALM 37:30 NCV

*Where jealousy and selfishness are, there will be confusion*
*and every kind of evil. But the wisdom that comes from God*
*is first of all pure, then peaceful, gentle, and easy to please.*
*This wisdom is always ready to help those who are troubled*
*and to do good for others. It is always fair and honest.*
JAMES 3:16-17 NCV

*If any of you is lacking in wisdom, ask God, who gives to all*
*generously and ungrudgingly, and it will be given you.*
JAMES 1:5 NRSV

# . . . I will pray.

Discerning Lord,

Confusion clouds my mind. I don't know how to deal with my child. I want to give up. Nothing I do or say seems to work. I've tried doing things on my own for so long, and it all ends up the same: a total mess.

I want to run away and forget that I'm a mom. Can't I disappear just for a while?

No, running away isn't the answer. I know I can't hide from my responsibilities or You. Instead, I bow my knees before You.

Forgive me, Lord, for not running to You first when confusion began to overtake me. I lack the wisdom to deal with my child in this situation, but I know I can find all the answers I need in You. When I'm on my knees, quiet before You, tuning out the advice of the world, I can hear Your voice. Confusion rages like a powerful tornado in my mind, but I seek shelter in Your wisdom. Thank You for calming the storm and clearing the air. I will rest in the peace Your wisdom brings.

Amen.

The greatest moments of your life are those when through all the confusion God got a message through to you plain and certain.

Bertha Munro

# When I'm worried about my child . . .

*[Jesus said] Not one sparrow (What do they cost?*
*Two for a penny?) can fall to the ground without your Father*
*knowing it. And the very hairs of your head are all*
*numbered. So don't worry! You are more valuable*
*to him than many sparrows.*
MATTHEW 10:29-31 TLB

*Don't fret or worry. Instead of worrying, pray. Let petitions*
*and praises shape your worries into prayers, letting God*
*know your concerns. Before you know it, a sense of God's*
*wholeness, everything coming together for good, will come and*
*settle you down. It's wonderful what happens when Christ*
*displaces worry at the center of your life.*
PHILIPPIANS 4:6-7 MSG

*Don't worry, because I am with you.*
*Don't be afraid, because I am your God.*
*I will make you strong and will help you;*
*I will support you with my right hand that saves you.*
ISAIAH 41:10 NCV

# . . . I will pray.

Comforting Lord,

"Hakuna Matata."

The song from *The Lion King* echoes through my brain. "No worries." I wish it were that easy. As a child I had no worries. But as an adult I gasp, thinking about all the things I am concerned about.

Every time my child leaves home to go to school or play down the street, I fret over all the things that could happen to her. Is she making the right choices? Will she be safe?

How can I not worry when the world around me seems to be self-destructing? I don't want my child to be taken down with the ills of the universe. Please help me learn to trust that You will keep her safe and guide her into Your truth.

Lord, I ask You to watch over my child and comfort my soul when she is away from me. Restore the peace of my youth and teach me how to trust You again as I did when I was a child. Quiet my soul and show me how to cast all my cares upon You. Help me not just to hum along to those carefree words, but to live them: "Hakuna Matata," no worries.

Thank You for that "problem-free philosophy."

Amen.

I am so made that worry and anxiety are sand in
the machinery of life: faith is oil.

E. Stanley Jones

God, be merciful to me;
On Thy grace I rest my plea;
In Thy vast, abounding grace,
My transgressions all erase.
Wash me wholly from my sin;
Cleanse from every ill within.

The Psalter

# Prayers
## of Confession

Lifting My Voice to God
When I Need Forgiveness

# When I'm too ambitious regarding my child . . .

*If you have bitter jealousy and selfish ambition in your heart,*
*do not be arrogant and so lie against the truth. This wisdom*
*is not that which comes down from above, but is earthly, nat-*
*ural. . . . The wisdom from above is first pure, then peace-*
*able, gentle, reasonable, full of mercy and good fruits.*

JAMES 3:14-15,17 NASB

*Do nothing out of selfish ambition or vain conceit,*
*but in humility consider others better than yourselves. . . .*
*Your attitude should be the same as that of Christ Jesus:*
*Who, being in the very nature God, did not consider equality*
*with God something to be grasped, but made himself nothing,*
*taking the very nature of a servant,*
*being made in human likeness.*

PHILIPPIANS 2:3,5-7

*Jesus said to the disciples, "If any of you wants to be my*
*follower, you must put aside your selfish ambition, shoulder*
*your cross, and follow me. If you try to keep your life for*
*yourself, you will lose it. But if you give up your life for me,*
*you will find true life. And how do you benefit if you gain the*
*whole world but lose your own soul in the process?*
*Is anything worth more than your soul?"*

MATTHEW 16:24-26 NLT

# . . . I will pray.

Loving God,

My child's ambition drives him to compete in all areas of his life. In school, if he receives less than an A, he feels like a failure. On the ball field, his anger rages at unfair calls.

Part of this is just his personality—the "type A" kid who never slows down. Another part of it is learned—from me. I have had such high hopes for him because he is so talented. Perhaps my ambitions have been too lofty.

God, forgive me for teaching my child that life is a race where he always needs to come in first. Forgive me for my overachieving attitude, for my soul that's never at rest or satisfied, that's always hoping, striving, and wanting more in my own life.

Lord, change me so I will be a better example to my child. Striving to be the best is admirable, but help both of us keep it in balance, remembering that our value is not based upon our performance. Help us to rest in Your unconditional love and to slow down enough to enjoy the journey—not simply strive for the blue ribbon. In Your eyes, we are always winners.

Amen.

The fruit of the Spirit is not push, drive, climb, grasp, and trample. . . . There is a legitimate place for blood, sweat, and tears; but it should have its roots in the call of God, not in the desire to get ahead. Life is more than a climb to the top of the heap.

Richard J. Foster

# When I've become angry with my child . . .

*Let everyone be quick to listen, slow to speak, slow to anger;*
*for your anger does not produce God's righteousness.*
JAMES 1:19-20 NRSV

✿

*If you are angry, don't sin by nursing your grudge. Don't let*
*the sun go down with you still angry—get over it quickly; for*
*when you are angry you give a mighty foothold to the devil.*
EPHESIANS 4:26-27 TLB

✿

*Self-control means controlling the tongue!*
*A quick retort can ruin everything.*
PROVERBS 13:3 TLB

✿

*A hot-tempered person starts fights and*
*gets into all kinds of sin.*
PROVERBS 29:22 NLT

✿

*Do not hasten in your spirit to be angry,*
*For anger rests in the bosom of fools.*
ECCLESIASTES 7:9 NKJV

# . . . I will pray.

Lord God,

It happened again this morning: I lost my temper. I ignored my child's misbehavior until it spun out of control and then I exploded. Sometimes my daughter doesn't see my anger coming. Other times it's all she sees. How can I allow myself to act that way?

Sometimes the fear in her eyes silences my anger. Other times it doesn't. I don't want my child to be afraid of me; I want her to love and respect me. I know You want me to respond to my child in love. Losing my temper doesn't strengthen our relationship. It wears it down—one bitter word at a time.

Lord, I can't tame my tongue on my own. I need Your help. Forgive me for letting my anger control my actions. Wash me clean of my sin and wipe the fright from my child's eyes and mind. Squelch the fire that burns in me when I feel the rage rising, and teach me positive ways to deal with my frustrations. Silence my inner voice that wants to scream. Replace it with Your calming Spirit, and help me use my tongue to build my child up instead of tear her down.

Amen.

When angry, take a lesson from technology;
always count down before blasting off.

Author Unknown

# When I've made foolish choices that affect my child . . .

Good leadership is a channel of water controlled by God;
he directs it to whatever ends he chooses.
PROVERBS 21:1 MSG

Happy are those who find wisdom,
and those who get understanding. . . .
Her ways are ways of pleasantness,
and all her paths are peace.
PROVERBS 3:13,17 NRSV

He shows how to distinguish right from wrong, how to find
the right decision every time. For wisdom and truth will enter
the very center of your being, filling your life with joy.
PROVERBS 2:9-10 TLB

❀

You are right and you do right, God;
your decisions are right on target.
PSALM 119:137 MSG

# . . . I will pray.

Heavenly Father,

Why is it so hard for me to say no to the things I know aren't the best for my child? I want him to be successful and excel in all areas of life, so I'm constantly signing him up for things he never asked to do. I just keep thinking that he'll enjoy them once he gets involved. The reality is that my doing so only adds stress to his life.

Why do I do such foolish things?

You'd think I'd have learned by now. I want to give my child everything he needs to be happy, but sometimes all he wants is to be with me, hanging out and having a little fun together instead of going to gymnastics or a music lesson.

Lord, I confess I've been foolish and have exasperated my child on more than one occasion. Forgive me for putting my own desire above his needs and not consulting You in these matters. Help me listen to what he wants and give me wisdom to choose, not just for him but for our entire family. Reveal to me when I'm making choices that are not consistent with Your will for our lives.

Amen.

God always gives his very best to those who
leave the choice with him.

James Hudson Taylor

# When I've become critical and judgmental toward my child . . .

*[Jesus said] Don't pick on people, jump on their failures, criticize their faults—unless, of course, you want the same treatment. That critical spirit has a way of boomeranging. It's easy to see a smudge on your neighbor's face and be oblivious to the ugly sneer on your own.*
MATTHEW 7:1-3 MSG

*The whole Law can be summed up in this one command: "Love others as you love yourself." But if instead of showing love among yourselves you are always critical and catty, watch out! Beware of ruining each other.*
GALATIANS 5:14-15 TLB

*Encourage one another and build up one another.*
1 THESSALONIANS 5:11 NASB

*Encourage one another day after day, as long as it is still called "Today," so that none of you will be hardened by the deceitfulness of sin.*
HEBREWS 3:13 NASB

# . . . I will pray.

Lord God,

I remember as a child hearing so much criticism from my parents. I'm sure they meant well, hoping to fix my problem areas and make me a better, stronger person. But it did just the opposite. It made me insecure and lonely. I vowed I would not make the same mistakes with my children—but I do. Especially with the one who is just like me.

I offer criticism when he fails, when what he really needs is encouragement. I give lectures instead of gentle answers to guide him. I'm a clanging gong in his ears when all he wants to hear is the sweet sound of my voice.

Father, forgive me for all the times I've failed and judged my child. More than anyone, I know how much criticism hurts. Lord, heal the insecurities of my heart so I can love and encourage my child. Help me to listen to him instead of cutting him off with bitter, critical words that only destroy. Thank You for intervening in this area of my life.

Amen.

By seeing the tremendous blossoming which a person can experience when surrounded by love and confidence, when he does not feel judged, we can measure the stifling power of other people's criticism.

Paul Tournier

# When my expectations are overwhelming my child . . .

*Don't make your children angry by the way you treat them.*
*Rather, bring them up with the discipline and*
*instruction approved by the Lord.*
EPHESIANS 6:4 NLT

*Do not exasperate your children,*
*so that they will not lose heart.*
COLOSSIANS 3:21 NASB

*As a father has compassion on his children,*
*so the LORD has compassion on those who fear him;*
*for he knows how we are formed,*
*he remembers that we are dust.*
PSALM 103:13-14

*When she speaks, her words are wise, and kindness is the*
*rule for everything she says. She watches carefully all that*
*goes on throughout her household, and is never lazy.*
*Her children stand and bless her.*
PROVERBS 31:26-28 TLB

# . . . I will pray.

Heavenly Father,

Today I made out my mental list and rattled off each point to my child in rapid succession. When he failed to follow through, I was annoyed that he'd forgotten to do half the things. In fact, I think he just tuned me out after the first couple of items.

Part of the problem is that he is only a child and his brain is wired differently from mine, yet I expect him to handle situations as I would. When he fails, I get upset. Why do I set him up for failure and myself up for disappointment?

God, forgive me for requiring my child to do more than he is capable of. Next time, remind me to make a shorter, more realistic list and to write down my expectations.

Heal the hurt inside of me, that space in my heart that feels the need to do everything perfectly and anything less is failure. Dig up the root that causes me to throw unrealistic goals at my child and help me see him through Your eyes. Teach me to have patience and show me how to manage my expectations so I don't exasperate him.

Amen.

While yielding to loving parental leadership,
children are also learning to yield to the
benevolent leadership of God himself.

James C. Dobson

# When I've failed to keep my word to my child . . .

*Keep your word even when it costs you.*
PSALM 15:4 MSG

*O God, . . . help me never to tell a lie.*
PROVERBS 30:7-8 TLB

*[The Lord commanded] If a man makes a promise to the*
*LORD or says he will do something special, he must keep his*
*promise. He must do what he said.*
NUMBERS 30:2 NCV

*If you do not make the promise, you will not be guilty.*
*You must do whatever you say you will do, because you chose*
*to make the promise to the LORD your God.*
DEUTERONOMY 23:22-23 NCV

*Love and truth form a good leader;*
*sound leadership is founded on loving integrity.*
PROVERBS 20:28 MSG

# . . . I will pray.

Heavenly Father,

She called me a liar again. But it wasn't a lie; we just ran out of time. I said we'd do something today, but other things came up and before I knew it, time had slipped away.

I admit this happens a lot. I tell my children they can have a treat or do something special. I really intend to follow through, but we all get busy and forget. When I do remember, circumstances frequently prevent my following through, and I'm branded a liar. Though I don't intentionally go against my word, to my children's hearts I've lied.

Lord, forgive me for the times I've failed to do what I've told my children we would do. Remind me not to make promises I can't keep. When my children ask for things, help me to think before I answer. Slow my response so I don't give a quick, easy yes. Instead, replace that word in my vocabulary with "We'll see" or "Maybe." Then when I have to say no, the disappointment won't be overwhelming. Restore my relationship and trust with my children. Thank You for mending this broken area of our lives.

Amen.

He who is slow in making a promise is most likely to
be faithful in the performance of it.

Jean-Jacques Rousseau

# When my personal habits are negatively affecting my child . . .

*[ Jesus said] I have set you an example that*
*you should do as I have done for you.*
JOHN 13:15

*Follow my example, as I follow the example of Christ.*
1 CORINTHIANS 11:1

*Set an example for the believers in speech, in life,*
*in love, in faith and in purity.*
1 TIMOTHY 4:12

*Be shepherds of God's flock that is under your care, serving as*
*overseers—not because you must, but because you are willing,*
*as God wants you to be;. . . eager to serve; not lording it over*
*those entrusted to you, but being examples to the flock.*
1 PETER 5:2-3

✿

*Behave carefully, taking life seriously. And here you yourself*
*must be an example to them of good deeds of every kind. Let*
*everything you do reflect your love of the truth.*
TITUS 2:6-7 TLB

# . . . I will pray.

Father God,

When I look at my child, I see myself. His loving heart reflects my own tenderness. I recognize my character strengths in the way he relates to others.

Yet, those are not the only ways in which he takes after me.

His impatience, anger, and lack of self-control also mirror the way I've been living my life lately. I can ignore the truth and put all the blame on him, or I can take responsibility for my words and actions.

He's living what he sees every day.

He's picking up my negative habits.

God, forgive me for behaving in a selfish way, for not realizing that my own personal habits are affecting my child negatively. Bring to the surface all the harmful things I do that affect his life and attitude, especially the ones I am blind to. Forgive me for letting my bad habits gain control of my life, and help me replace them with good ones. Make me a positive role model, one my son can emulate and be proud of. Thank You for seeing me as I can be, not as I am right now.

Amen.

Sow an act and you reap a habit.
Sow a habit and you reap a character.
Sow a character and you reap a destiny.
Samuel Smiles

When I've told lies to
control my child . . .

*If we confess our sins, he who is faithful and just will
forgive us our sins and cleanse us.*
1 JOHN 1:9 NRSV

*Do not lie to one another, since you laid aside the old self
with its evil practices, and have put on the new self.*
COLOSSIANS 3:9-10 NASB

*[Wisdom cries]
Listen, for I have worthy things to say;
I open my lips to speak what is right.
My mouth speaks what is true,
for my lips detest wickedness.
All the words of my mouth are just;
none of them is crooked or perverse.*
PROVERBS 8:6-8

*She speaks with wisdom,
and faithful instruction is on her tongue.*
PROVERBS 31:26

# . . . I will pray.

Heavenly Father,

While waiting in line at the store today, my child's anger raged out of control. So I told a lie to calm her down. I feel so guilty about it now. Why would I say such a thing?

I don't consider myself a liar.

In fact, I don't tolerate it when my children keep the truth from me. Even a "little white lie" is still a lie, isn't it?

How many times have I told my child the kiddie ride at the store was broken, just so we wouldn't have to stop and ride it? Or the bakery didn't have her favorite cookie because I didn't want her to get chocolate on her dress?

God, forgive me for lying to my child, for thinking my deception was okay. At the time of my sin, I didn't feel that I was doing anything wrong, but I know Your way is better. Help me speak the truth to my child in a way she can understand and accept instead of manipulating her behavior with my lies. Give me a wise word that will achieve what I'm trying to accomplish with my child.

Thank You for Your forgiveness that releases me from my guilt and shame.

Amen.

Love the truth though it may do you harm;
hate the lie though it may please you.

Arabian Proverb

# When I've been prideful and arrogant toward my child . . .

*I, the prisoner of the Lord, implore you to walk in a manner*
*worthy of the calling with which you have been called, with*
*all humility and gentleness, with patience, showing tolerance*
*for one another in love, being diligent to preserve the unity of*
*the Spirit in the bond of peace.*
EPHESIANS 4:1-3 NASB

*All of you, clothe yourselves with humility toward one*
*another, because, "God opposes the proud*
*but gives grace to the humble."*
1 PETER 5:5

*Love cares more for others than for self. . . .*
*Love doesn't strut,*
*Doesn't have a swelled head,*
*Doesn't force itself on others,*
*Isn't always "me first,"*
*Doesn't fly off the handle.*
1 CORINTHIANS 13:4-5 MSG

*First pride, then the crash—*
*the bigger the ego, the harder the fall.*
PROVERBS 16:18 MSG

# . . . I will pray.

Lord of Heaven,

My child is maturing in ways I'm not ready for. I still see him as that stubborn little boy resistant to bedtime. Yet, he's not my baby anymore. He has his own personality, his own mind. He's bright, sensitive, and opinionated, yet he still needs guidance and discipline.

How do I balance his desires with my responsibility as his mother?

He says I never listen to him, that I cut him off in midsentence. And he's right. I have caught myself doing that. Forgive me for dominating him, for silencing his voice and feeling that because I'm his mother I have the right to control his thoughts and actions. I can't control them; I can only guide them.

If my child feels he's not being heard, he will never hear me. Remind me to listen to what he has to say, and put a guard over my tongue so I won't cut him off. Help me to swallow my pride and treat him with respect. I apologize for being arrogant. Show me when my pride is getting in the way of our relationship, so I can replace it with humility.

Thank You, Lord, for catching me when I fall.

Amen.

Humility is strong—not bold;
quiet—not speechless; sure—not arrogant.

Estelle Smith

# When I've sinned (broken God's laws) in regard to my child . . .

*[Jesus said] If you are standing before the altar in the Temple, offering a sacrifice to God, and suddenly remember that a friend has something against you, leave your sacrifice there beside the altar and go and apologize and be reconciled to him, and then come and offer your sacrifice to God. Come to terms quickly.*

MATTHEW 5:23-25 TLB

*Be angry but do not sin; do not let the sun go down on your anger, and do not make room for the devil.*

EPHESIANS 4:26-27 NRSV

*[Peter said] Everyone who believes in him receives forgiveness of sins through his name.*

ACTS 10:43 NRSV

❀

*"Blessed are those whose iniquities are forgiven, and whose sins are covered; blessed is the one against whom the Lord will not reckon sin."*

ROMANS 4:7-8 NRSV

# . . . I will pray.

Gracious Lord,

I wounded my child's spirit today. As her anger grew out of control, I felt those cutting words forming on my tongue. Her complaining wore me down; it was more than I could take. I let the painful words fly. It was wrong. I've sinned against You and my child. Please, forgive me.

I know anger is a normal emotion. Jesus felt it, but in His anger He never sinned. When does my anger cross over into sin? When I hurt others. When my words cause my child a hurt that cannot be erased but only lessened through my apology.

I asked my child to forgive me. She did and we hugged. Yet, I wish I hadn't let my anger hurt her. I'm her mother. I love her. I should be nurturing and patient, not intolerant and mean.

Lord, help me to recognize the triggers that cause me to sin. Give me the self-control to stop anger before it crosses the line. When I fail, comfort my child and help me reconcile our relationship quickly. Thank You for being the God of forgiveness.

Amen.

An apology is saying the right thing after
doing the wrong thing.

Author Unknown

# When I've neglected my responsibilities to my child . . .

*Shepherd God's flock, for whom you are responsible.*
*Watch over them because you want to, not because you are*
*forced. . . . Do it because you are happy to serve.*
1 PETER 5:2 NCV

*[The Lord] said to me, "My grace is sufficient for you, for my*
*power is made perfect in weakness." Therefore I will boast all*
*the more gladly about my weaknesses, so that Christ's power*
*may rest on me. . . . For when I am weak, then I am strong.*
2 CORINTHIANS 12:9-10

*He gives power to the tired and worn out, and strength to*
*the weak. Even the youths shall be exhausted, and the young*
*men will all give up. But they that wait upon the Lord*
*shall renew their strength. They shall mount up with*
*wings like eagles; they shall run and not be weary;*
*they shall walk and not faint.*
ISAIAH 40:29-31 TLB

# . . . I will pray.

Gracious Father,

So much for being Super Mom. The oil on the van needs to be changed. Laundry procreates faster than the bunnies under our lilac bush. A novel beckons me. Television seems blissfully mindless. Above it all the clamor of the children hovers like the insistent drone of mosquitoes at dusk. I don't want to be a mom today.

I know You've seen me, but I want to confess to You anyway. I've settled squabbles by bellowing instructions from my position on the couch, drilled out marching orders in the face of precious requests: "Watch me, Mommy!" "Will you play with us now?" I've slouched on the sidelines of their games, their energy, and their poignant demands. And I'm sorry.

Nudge me when I'm tempted to neglect my responsibilities. Summon my playful spirit, so I can participate in their childhood with joy. I grew up asking to be a mommy someday. What a privilege it is, even though some days the load is just too much for me.

Thank You for being the God of second chances. Allow me to rest in the sweet thought that as long as I am given breath, there is tomorrow.

Amen.

Do right, and God's recompense to you will be
the power to do more right.

Frederick William Robertson

# When I need to be in right relationship with God . . .

*[ Jesus said] Look! I have been standing at the door and
I am constantly knocking. If anyone hears me calling him
and opens the door, I will come in and
fellowship with him and he with me.*
REVELATION 3:20 TLB

*Your fellowship with God enables you to
gain a victory over the Evil One.*
1 JOHN 2:14 MSG

*Draw near to God and he will draw near to you.*
JAMES 4:8 RSV

*Now we can rejoice in our wonderful new relationship with
God—all because of what our Lord Jesus Christ has done for
us in making us friends of God.*
ROMANS 5:11 NLT

*Cultivate your own relationship with God.*
ROMANS 14:22 MSG

# . . . I will pray.

Holy God,

This morning my preschooler brought me a crumpled T-shirt. "Mommy, this shirt feels funny. Could you inside-out it for me?" Right now I feel just like that shirt. Rumpled. Scratchy. Out of sorts. Like life is fitting me wrong. I know why. I haven't made time for You.

There's that old saying, "If you aren't as close to God as you once were, who moved?" I know it wasn't You, Father, but the press of life feels crushing. I am ruled by the tyranny of the urgent.

I know that I really am too busy not to pray. Nudge me throughout the day. Whisper to me on the breeze. Smile at me through the brilliant colors of the tulips that line our walkway. Call me to spend time with You as the stars come out to play. Beckon to me each evening to spend time reading *The Greatest Story Ever Told*.

Light in me a holy passion, a fire that burns from being in Your presence. Remind me that only by being consumed by You can I avoid burnout. I don't want to live life inside out, so I humbly ask You to inside-out me too.

Amen.

When he says to your disturbed, distracted, restless soul or mind, "Come unto me," he is saying, come out of the strife and doubt and struggle of what is at the moment. . . . into that which was and is and is to be—the eternal, the essential, the absolute.

Phillips Brooks

# When I've been unforgiving toward my child . . .

*Never seek revenge or bear a grudge against anyone, but love*
*your neighbor as yourself. I am the LORD.*
LEVITICUS 19:18 NLT

❁

*[Jesus said] When you are praying, first forgive anyone*
*you are holding a grudge against, so that your*
*Father in heaven will forgive your sins, too.*
MARK 11:25 NLT

❁

*[The Lord] never bears a grudge, nor remains angry forever.*
PSALM 103:9 TLB

❁

*[Love] does not hold grudges.*
1 CORINTHIANS 13:5 TLB

❁

*Be gentle and ready to forgive; never hold grudges.*
*Remember, the Lord forgave you, so you must forgive others.*
COLOSSIANS 3:13 TLB

# . . . I will pray.

God, my Father,

My daughter has hurt my feelings. I feel unappreciated, taken for granted.

This rudeness—from the child that I birthed, rocked, read to, chauffeured, and taught to ride a bike—was unexpected. Now I'm nursing a grudge.

I asked for a respectful tone of voice; I got eyes rolled to the ceiling, foot stomping, and huffy breathing. My ears are still ringing from the upstairs bedroom door slamming.

The hour is late and I'm still washing clothes, cleaning the kitchen, paying the bills—trying to scrape together money for braces, ballet, and the latest jeans. Right now, I feel resentful.

Then, in these quiet minutes before bedtime, a bouncing ponytail and two penitent eyes peer around the corner. A softer voice sheepishly inquires, "Mom, can we talk?"

I know she wants to be forgiven; her hunched shoulders and slouched posture speak of regret. But I'm not sure I'm there yet.

God, help my heart be tender. Remind me that I will be forgiven only as I forgive others and that I am to model forgiveness for my child.

Help me go to her, arms—and heart—outstretched. Thank You for Your mercy that runs after me.

Amen.

Forgiveness is a required course.

Charles R. Swindoll

Make me an intercessor,
One who can really pray,
One of "the Lord's remembrancers"
By night as well as day.

Frances Ridley Havergal

# Prayers
# of Intercession

Lifting My Voice to God
on Behalf of Others

# When my child is struggling with addiction . . .

*Sin will have no dominion over you,*
*since you are . . . under grace.*
ROMANS 6:14 RSV

*[The Lord] sent from on high, He took me;*
*He drew me out of many waters.*
*He delivered me from my strong enemy,*
*And from those who hated me,*
*for they were too mighty for me.*
PSALM 18:16-17 NASB

*On God rests my deliverance and my honor;*
*my mighty rock, my refuge is God.*
PSALM 62:7 RSV

*Behold, the eye of the Lord is on those who fear Him,*
*On those who hope in His mercy,*
*To deliver their soul from death,*
*And to keep them alive in famine.*
PSALM 33:18-19 NKJV

# . . . I will pray.

O God,

My heart is breaking!

I thought we had done everything right: helping with D.A.R.E. homework, the talks about the dangers of drugs, respecting the wonder of our bodies as God's creation, keeping alcohol out of our home.

But it seems that peer pressure has won out over parental influence. It started out innocently at first—"Just seeing what it was like," he said—but it didn't stop there. Then came the lies. Now his body craves those things, as when he as a toddler craved crackers and juice. I am terrified; my world is spinning out of control. I beseech You for his deliverance.

Calm my spirit. Rescue me from deep doubts and self-blame. Remind me that life has never been under my control, but under Yours. My child says he wants to change, God. Give him the grace to do so. I ask You to give me vigilance and special discernment to know when things are amiss. Guide us through the process of rebuilding trust. Grant us hope. Help me to know that addiction is strong, but it is not stronger than You.

I thank You for being our Deliverer.

Amen.

Father, set me free in the glory of thy will,
so that I will only as thou willest. . . . Thou alone art
deliverance—absolute safety from every cause and
kind of trouble that ever existed, anywhere now exists,
or ever can exist in thy universe.

George MacDonald

# When my child does not respect authority . . .

*Let no one despise your youth,*
*but be an example to the believers in word,*
*in conduct, in love, in spirit, in faith, in purity.*
1 TIMOTHY 4:12 NKJV

*Run away from the evil young people like to do.*
*Try hard to live right and to have faith, love, and peace,*
*together with those who trust in the Lord from pure hearts.*
*Stay away from foolish and stupid arguments, because you*
*know they grow into quarrels. And a servant of the Lord*
*must not quarrel but must be kind to everyone.*
2 TIMOTHY 2:22-24 NCV

*Give respect and honor to all to whom it is due.*
ROMANS 13:7 NLT

*We ask you to appreciate those who work hard among you,*
*who lead you in the Lord and teach you. Respect them with a*
*very special love because of the work they do.*
1 THESSALONIANS 5:12-13 NCV

# . . . I will pray.

Precious Lord,

Why is it that teenagers think they know everything? Lately life has become one continuous battle. My child's outbursts sound like a toddler crying out for independence, "You're not my boss!" Only at this age, it's not so cute.

There are the other familiar phrases too:

"Why can't I? Everyone else gets to."

"You guys are ruining my life!"

"When I have kids, I'm never going to. . . ."

Then today came the call from school asking me to meet with the principal about my child's increasing insolence. Insolence? My sweet child? My mind floods with images of earlier times. Unprompted thanks. Precocious smiles. Willing obedience.

Help me not to hang on too tightly to the past. Allow me to see my child for the adult she is becoming. Guide me so I model respect for authority too: speed limits, taking only the correct number of items to the express lane at the grocery store. And most of all, help me show respect for You. Bless me with both firm resolve and heaps of humor.

Thank You that this, too, shall pass.

Amen.

Parents take small, self-centered monsters, who spend much of their time screaming defiantly and hurling peas on the carpet, and teach them to share, to wait their turn, to respect others' property. These lessons translate into respect for others, self-restraint, obedience to law.

Charles Colson

When my child is afraid . . .

The LORD is my light and my salvation;
whom shall I fear?
The LORD is the stronghold of my life;
of whom shall I be afraid?

PSALM 27:1 RSV

God is our protection and our strength.
He always helps in times of trouble.
So we will not be afraid even if the earth shakes.

PSALM 46:1-2 NCV

We live within the shadow of the Almighty, sheltered by the
God who is above all gods. This I declare, that he alone is my
refuge, my place of safety; he is my God, and I am trusting
him. For he rescues you from every trap, and protects you
from the fatal plague. He will shield you with his wings!
They will shelter you. His faithful promises are your armor.

PSALM 91:1-4 TLB

# . . . I will pray.

Father God,

From the moment Adam and Eve disobeyed You, fear entered the human heart. It is so easy for my child—and me—to be caught up in fear, to imagine the worst, to dwell in it.

But, God, I know that is not Your plan for us. Because of Your faithful protection, we can lie down and sleep in peace. You are the Author of Peace, the Calmer of storms, the Final Authority on everything.

Father, reach into my child's tangled fears and borrowed troubles and replace them with Your wonderful peace. As You calmed the storm on the seas, calm the storms that whip her mind into waves of worry. Guard her thoughts, even in sleep.

In Your Word, the psalmist ran to You when he was afraid and put his trust in You. Let my example teach her to go to You whenever she is afraid. As she is clinging to me, let me show her how to cling to You.

Amen.

❖

Fear makes the wolf bigger than he is.

German Proverb

# When my child has anger issues . . .

Sometimes mere words are not enough—discipline is needed.
For the words may not be heeded.
PROVERBS 29:19 TLB

Patience is better than strength.
Controlling your temper is better than capturing a city.
PROVERBS 16:32 NCV

Put these things out of your life: anger, bad temper,
doing or saying things to hurt others.
COLOSSIANS 3:8 NCV

A quietly given gift soothes an irritable person;
a heartfelt present cools a hot temper.
PROVERBS 21:14 MSG

Bad temper is contagious—
don't get infected.
PROVERBS 22:24-25 MSG

# . . . I will pray.

Holy God,

Lately it seems as though my child explodes at the slightest provocation. He demands his own way, refuses to share, and his memory of real or imagined slights is long. He's become a champion grudge-holder.

It hurts me when I hear him say, "I'll get back at them, and I'll never forget what they did," or "She did it to me first."

His hands have even reached out to slap in anger.

God, we do not consciously teach our children to behave this way, but perhaps our own negative reactions have spoken far louder than our family devotions. Be quick to listen, slow to speak, and slow to become angry—surely those are some of Your hardest teachings. Forgive me for letting my anger get the best of me and for setting a poor example.

Give me wisdom to help my child break his habit of anger. Begin by changing me. On a daily basis, show me healthier ways to respond so I can instruct my son in dealing with disappointments, delays, and frustrations. Help both of us learn to react as You would.

Thank You for being such a good Teacher.

Amen.

Don't get angry at the person who
acts in ways that displease you.
Give him the smile he lacks. Spread the sunshine
of your Lord's limitless love.

Joni Eareckson Tada

# When my child asks for answers . . .

*After three days [ Jesus' parents] found Him in the temple,*
*sitting in the midst of the teachers, both listening to them and*
*asking them questions. And all who heard Him were amazed*
*at His understanding and His answers.*
LUKE 2:46-47 NASB

*I am teaching you true and reliable words*
*so that you can give true answers to anyone who asks.*
PROVERBS 22:21 NCV

*Oh, the depth of the riches both of the wisdom and knowledge*
*of God! How unsearchable are His judgments and*
*unfathomable His ways!*
ROMANS 11:33 NASB

*The LORD gives wisdom;*
*From His mouth come knowledge and understanding.*
PROVERBS 2:6 NKJV

# . . . I will pray.

Omniscient Father,

My child has so many questions. Some are simple, while others are quite deep. "How can God be everywhere at once?" "Does He really listen to me pray since all the people in that hurricane need Him too?" "Does God ever get sleepy?" "Who created God?"

The parade of questions seems endless and often unanswerable. Like King Solomon, I ask You only for wisdom. To be able to answer truthfully. To admit the gaps in my knowledge and to be humble enough to search for the answers together.

Replace my feelings of inadequacy with quiet confidence in You.

Our time together under one roof is limited. One day the nest will be empty, and these deep talks, the true baring of souls, will be but a memory. These times are sacred. Help me to make the best use of the opportunities I am given to share You with him.

I ask You to fill my child's mind with hunger for Your Word and assurance that You hold the answer to every question he will ever have. Because You are everywhere and know everything, I can release this burden to You.

Amen.

Heaven is the place where questions
and answers become one.

Elie Wiesel

# When my child is struggling with my beliefs . . .

*I pray for you constantly, asking God,*
*the glorious Father of our Lord Jesus Christ,*
*to give you wisdom to see clearly and really understand*
*who Christ is and all that he has done for you.*

EPHESIANS 1:16-17 TLB

*Faith comes from hearing the Good News, and people hear*
*the Good News when someone tells them about Christ.*

ROMANS 10:17 NCV

*Jesus said to him, "If you can believe, all things are possible to*
*him who believes." Immediately the father of the child cried*
*out and said with tears, "Lord, I believe; help my unbelief!"*

MARK 9:23-24 NKJV

*Your godly lives will speak to them better than any words.*
*They will be won over by watching your pure, godly behavior.*

1 PETER 3:1-2 NLT

# . . . I will pray.

Father in Heaven,

I am weary and confused, and my soul feels weighted down. It seems as if once again Christianity is on trial. The media, school texts, and popular TV shows all contradict our faith. Messages of mediocrity and compromise chase my child. Against all the images, all the arguments, all the court hoopla, the case for belief in You gets harder to make. Sometimes my child wonders if what we've told him is right.

God, I ask You to help me reassure my child that prayer works, that miracles are real. Show him evidence and examples as You touch his life and are present in daily details. Give me wisdom, real life stories, and appropriate scriptures to share. Convict my child of the certainty that Your Word can be trusted in its entirety.

God, these are pivotal days for my impressionable child's faith. Mold him into who You've designed him to be. Remind him that he is Your child, known and planned by You before one of his days came to be. Make Yourself real to him and reveal the miracle of Your creation to him each day.

Thank You for being who You say You are.

Amen.

God takes and God keeps the initiative.
God alone can make a man a believer,
Our part is to accept or reject his initiative.

John Powell

# When my child needs to make good choices . . .

Teach your children to choose the right path,
and when they are older, they will remain upon it.
<small>PROVERBS 22:6 NLT</small>

I have set before you life or death, blessing or curse. Oh, that
you would choose life; that you and your children might live!
Choose to love the Lord your God and to obey him and to
cling to him, for he is your life and the length of your days.
<small>DEUTERONOMY 30:19-20 TLB</small>

Words kill, words give life; they're either poison or fruit
—you choose.
<small>PROVERBS 18:21 MSG</small>

Who are they that fear the LORD?
He will teach them the way that they should choose.
<small>PSALM 25:12 NRSV</small>

I have chosen the way of truth;
Your judgments I have laid before me.
<small>PSALM 119:30 NKJV</small>

# . . . I will pray.

Loving Father,

Kids have to make such tough choices these days. I'm excited to see my child growing up, while at the same time I am terrified by the dangers lurking around every corner. Along with an elevated sense of maturity, he will likely have opportunities to turn away from what he knows to be true and right. He might be offered drugs. Sexual exploration runs rampant. Foul language abounds. Words that were considered taboo not long ago are now blurted out on TV during the family hour.

Father, You are a parent too. You knew when You sent Your Son to earth that He would face temptations and choices. You knew He would be despised and rejected for showing Your light to the world. I am profoundly grateful that You understand the pride I have in my son as well as my concerns for him.

I'm praying that You will walk with my child where I cannot. When he is presented with opportunities to make choices, I pray that You will strengthen him so he will choose well. Surround him with godly friends who will support his values, and deliver him from evil.

Amen.

God asks no one whether he will accept life.
This is not the choice.
The only choice you have as you go through life
is how you will live it.

Bernard Meltzer

# When my child is dealing with conflict . . .

*Christ, who suffered for you, is your example.*
*Follow in his steps. He never sinned, and he never deceived*
*anyone. He did not retaliate when he was insulted. When he*
*suffered, he did not threaten to get even. He left his case in*
*the hands of God, who always judges fairly.*

1 PETER 2:21-23 NLT

*Don't repay evil for evil. Don't retaliate when people say*
*unkind things about you. Instead, pay them back with a*
*blessing. That is what God wants you to do, and he will bless*
*you for it. For the Scriptures say, "If you want a happy life*
*and good days, keep your tongue from speaking evil,*
*and keep your lips from telling lies. Turn away from evil*
*and do good. Work hard at living in peace with others.*
*The eyes of the Lord watch over those who do right,*
*and his ears are open to their prayers."*

1 PETER 3:9-12 NLT

*"Here is a simple, rule-of-thumb guide for behavior: Ask*
*yourself what you want people to do for you, then grab the*
*initiative and do it for them. Add up God's Law and*
*Prophets and this is what you get.*

MATTHEW 7:12 MSG

# . . . I will pray.

My Redeemer,

"Sticks and stones may break my bones, but words will never hurt me." Oh, God, it's simply not true! I'm surprised at how personally I feel all of my child's struggles. Lately, I've wanted to march onto the school playground and save her, just like Wonder Woman.

Of course I know that wouldn't really solve anything, but often my child comes home in tears, feeling picked on, excluded, and ridiculed. Making friends, learning new concepts at school, competing in sports, and learning to be responsible can be overwhelming to a child. Conflict with peers makes it even harder.

You've dealt with Your share of bullies, and You have always championed the underdog. I pray for Your intervention for my child, that You will turn this situation around for her. I pray that You will give her favor with the children, teachers, and coaches who cross her path. Help me teach her godly ways to respond, how to gently deflect hurtful comments. Reassure her of Your love, and keep her self-image strong. Show me where I need to become involved and how.

Thank You, Father, for always being that faithful Friend who sticks closer than a brother.

Amen.

Never wrestle with a pig. You both get all dirty,
and the pig likes it.

Author Unknown

# When my child is in danger . . .

*During danger he will keep me safe in his shelter.*
*He will hide me in his Holy Tent,*
*or he will keep me safe on a high mountain.*
Psalm 27:5 ncv

✿

*The* Lord *is your protection;*
*you have made God Most High your place of safety.*
*Nothing bad will happen to you;*
*no disaster will come to your home.*
Psalm 91:9-10 ncv

✿

*The* Lord *will protect you from all dangers;*
*he will guard your life.*
*The* Lord *will guard you as you come and go,*
*both now and forever.*
Psalm 121:7-8 ncv

*Do not be afraid of sudden fear*
*Nor of the onslaught of the wicked when it comes;*
*For the* Lord *will be your confidence*
*And will keep your foot from being caught.*
Proverbs 3:25-26 nasb

# . . . I will pray.

Precious Savior,

Children face so many more dangers these days than when I was a child. Abductions, abuse, and the proffering of drugs are on the rise. Everything from gangs to bad language threatens to leap out at my child. The world lays out a veritable buffet of inappropriate choices.

I look out the window at the darkening sky and the heightening wind. It seems a perfect match for the potential dangers that swirl around my mind. God, I'm frightened. Whenever danger threatens or even lurks in my imagination, my most primal instincts overtake me and I want to be there holding her.

I pray for Your protection for my child. Walk with her when I cannot go along. Whisper Your wisdom to her when I am not there. Help her to see You as her best Friend, her Confidante, and yes, her Protector.

I ask Your physical protection around her too. Thank You for the angels that You've assigned to her. Guide her safely, champion her cause. Give her generous doses of Your wisdom. Lend her Your insight. Protect her in every way—spirit, soul, and body.

Thank You for protecting my child.

Amen.

Believing God's promises the Christian is taken
through difficulties of every shape and size
—and arrives safely.

Richard C. Halverson

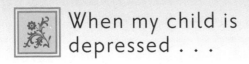

# When my child is depressed . . .

*My soul melts from heaviness;*
*Strengthen me according to Your word.*
PSALM 119:28 NKJV

✿

*Come quickly, Lord, and answer me, for my depression*
*deepens; don't turn away from me or I shall die. . . . Lead me*
*in good paths, for your Spirit is good.*
PSALM 143:7,10 TLB

✿

*Anxiety in the heart of man causes depression,*
*But a good word makes it glad.*
PROVERBS 12:25 NKJV

✿

*The Spirit of the Lord GOD is upon Me, . . .*
*To console those who mourn in Zion,*
*To give them beauty for ashes,*
*The oil of joy for mourning,*
*The garment of praise for the spirit of heaviness.*
ISAIAH 61:1,3 NKJV

# . . . I will pray.

Great Counselor, Mighty God,

My child seems to be stuck in depression, and I don't know what to do. He mopes, sulks, and spends most of his time sitting in his room. Even his once gargantuan appetite has dwindled. Nothing I have tried seems to do more than bring temporary respite.

I'm not sure what has brought about this season of depression, wrapping him in its ugly blanket. Sitting on the bench for one too many games? A scolding from his teacher about a late paper? Rejection by a girl or one of his peers? A chemical imbalance? Whatever it is, You know, and I find comfort in that.

Father, I ask You to work on his heart from the inside. Lift up his head, restore his hope. Perhaps the key is for him to reach out to someone else in need. If so, bring that person to his mind.

If there is anything else I should do, reveal it to me. In the meantime, may our unconditional love, the passage of time, and Your "unforced rhythms of grace" (Matthew 11:29 MSG) bring him around. Help me to model optimism and cheerfulness without irritating him.

Thank You for being the Author of joy!

Amen.

Earth hath no sorrow that heaven cannot heal.

Thomas Moore

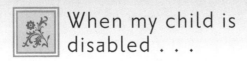# When my child is
disabled . . .

*When my anxious thoughts multiply within me,*
*Your consolations delight my soul.*

*"I know the plans I have for you," declares the LORD, "plans*
*to prosper you and not to harm you, plans to give you hope*
*and a future."*

*Thus says the LORD, your Redeemer, the Holy One of Israel,*
*"I am the LORD your God, who teaches you to profit,*
*Who leads you in the way you should go."*

🌸

*A man's gift makes room for him*
*and brings him before great men.*

# . . . I will pray.

Father God,

Through the window, I watch the other children play—each giggle, each kick of a ball, each swing of a bat, each exuberant run shredding my heart. Why, I wonder for the umpteenth time, won't my little child ever be able to play like that? I choke down a rising sense of bitterness and injustice along with my cooling coffee. You didn't create children to be bound by disability.

Forgive me, Father, for even as I curb my desire to rant and rave, I am mindful of so many other blessings: a supportive church family, play dates with fun friends from the neighborhood, a society that is more accepting and accommodating of people with disabilities. Thank You for a great school education, opportunities to participate in sports through organizations such as the Special Olympics. A child who is otherwise in good health.

Father, I pray that you would help me discern and encourage his special gifts and talents. That You would lead us to other families who are in the same situation as we are, that he would find Christian friends there. Keep us mindful that You have a plan for our lives and that Your strength shines in our weakness.

Thank You that someday we will all have perfect bodies.

Amen.

❖

Keep your face to the sunshine and
you cannot see the shadow.

Helen Adams Keller

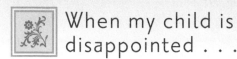# When my child is disappointed . . .

Come, Lord, and show me your mercy, for I am helpless,
overwhelmed, in deep distress; my problems go from
bad to worse. Oh, save me from them all!
See my sorrows; feel my pain.
PSALM 25:16-18 TLB

You keep track of all my sorrows.
You have collected all my tears in your bottle.
You have recorded each one in your book.
PSALM 56:8 NLT

❉

Thus says the LORD,
". . . Remember not the former things,
nor consider the things of old.
Behold, I am doing a new thing;
now it springs forth, do you not perceive it?
I will make a way in the wilderness
and rivers in the desert."
ISAIAH 43:14,18-19 RSV

❉

Many are the afflictions of the righteous,
But the LORD delivers him out of them all.
PSALM 34:19 NASB

# . . . I will pray.

Dear Father, Mender of Broken Hearts,

Disappointment is part of life, but my heart aches for my child. The downcast expression on her face tears at my insides. Where is that twinkle in her eyes? I pray for words aptly spoken to encourage her. I ask You to give her that treasured quality of resilience that she might learn to bounce back, both now and whenever life hands her less than she wants.

I am reminded of that old English proverb that says each cloud has a silver lining. Or as Annie of the Broadway play would sing, "The sun'll come out tomorrow." Indeed, Your Word reminds us that weeping may remain for a night, but joy comes in the morning. (Psalm 30:5.) Cause something good to come from this situation. Restore that familiar brightness to my child's eyes, and strengthen her with Your joy. Grace her with optimism. Lead her to examples of greatness born of adversity, and remind her of the value of perseverance and the satisfaction of overcoming trouble with hard work.

Most of all, remind her that You love granting the desires of our hearts and that many other opportunities will come her way.

Amen.

Out of every disappointment there is treasure.
Satan whispers, "All is lost."
God says, "Much can be gained."

Frances J. Roberts

# When my child needs discipline . . .

*Discipline always seems painful rather than pleasant at the time, but later it yields the peaceful fruit of righteousness to those who have been trained by it.*

HEBREWS 12:11 NRSV

*The LORD corrects those he loves, just as parents correct the child they delight in.*

PROVERBS 3:12 NCV

*Intelligent children listen to their parents; foolish children do their own thing. . . . A refusal to correct is a refusal to love; love your children by disciplining them.*

PROVERBS 13:1,24 MSG

*Discipline your children while you still have the chance; indulging them destroys them.*

PROVERBS 19:18 MSG

# . . . I will pray.

Precious Father,

How I wish I could travel back in time to visit with Joseph and Mary. Perfect Jesus didn't need discipline, but surely James and the others did. I know Your Word says that You discipline those You love. I also know that allowing my child free rein would be to fail as a parent.

But sometimes I am too tired for discipline. Other times I feel guilt over working long hours, so I give in. Keep me consistent so that tiredness, dejection, or frustrations don't cloud my decisions.

Help me distinguish between punishment and discipline. Guide me so I don't act out of anger, but from a heart of love. Help me to be creative and proactive, so I am not simply responding to crises.

God, I want to remember that the challenges, joys, and irritations of parenting are all privileges. I want You to diligently remind me that these years are all too fleeting and that someday I will miss things that seem so daily to me now.

More than anything, I want my child to grow up to be like You. Thank You for Your example as a loving, patient, and perfect Parent.

Amen.

Discipline and love are not antithetical;
one is a function of the other.

James C. Dobson

# When my child is torn by divorce . . .

*A father to the fatherless, a defender of widows,*
*is God in his holy dwelling.*
*God sets the lonely in families.*
PSALM 68:5-6

*Vindicate the weak and fatherless;*
*Do justice to the afflicted and destitute.*
PSALM 82:3 NASB

*He defends the orphans and widows,*
*but he blocks the way of the wicked.*
PSALM 146:9 NCV

*The LORD is near to those who have a broken heart,*
*And saves such as have a contrite spirit.*
PSALM 34:18 NKJV

# . . . I will pray.

O God,

The children found me this afternoon, sitting on my closet floor, sobbing. I hadn't wanted them to know I was crying; they need me to be strong. I gathered them tightly to me, hoping my presence would be a tangible comfort.

I watch them and my heart breaks when they playact divorce with their G.I. Joes and ragtag collection of legless Barbies, whose too-bright smiles and fancy dresses belie their true condition. That's how I feel too.

Guard my mouth. Don't let my words encourage bitterness in them; keep it from me too. Help me exhibit Your strength without being stoic. To be optimistic while acknowledging reality.

By Your grace, help us build new memories and a strong family, even without the physical presence of their dad. Remind me and my children that You set the lonely in families.

I ask You for special wisdom that will allow me to sense what my children need. I pray that they might learn to trust You with their hurt feelings on sad days and that they would learn this by watching me.

Thank You for being my Husband and a Father to the fatherless.

Amen.

When God sees a scar, . . . he creates a star!

Robert Harold Schuller

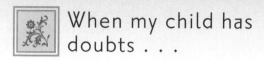

# When my child has doubts . . .

*By awesome deeds in righteousness You will answer us,*
*O God of our salvation,*
*You who are the confidence of all the ends of the earth.*

PSALM 65:5 NKJV

✿

*The LORD will be your confidence,*
*And will keep your foot from being caught.*

PROVERBS 3:26 NKJV

✿

*In the fear of the LORD one has strong confidence.*

PROVERBS 14:26 RSV

✿

*Thus says the Lord GOD, the Holy One of Israel:*
*". . . In quietness and confidence shall be your strength."*

ISAIAH 30:15 NKJV

✿

*When I am afraid, I will put my confidence in you.*
*Yes, I will trust the promises of God.*

PSALM 56:3-4 TLB

# . . . I will pray.

My Solid Rock,

Sometimes it seems that confidence is such a shaky thing and praise ephemeral. One day my child soars, confident in his abilities, his friends, his relationship with You, and his future plans. Other days that same child is assailed with doubts. He worries about being good enough. His friends seem fickle. He is unsure about his future.

I ask that You show Yourself to my child as he teeters on the ledge between childhood and being grown-up. Just as he learned to walk with baby steps, help him to take steps toward You for his confidence. Let his esteem and his future plans rest wholly in You. Lead him toward activities he can excel in and to friends who will support his walk with You.

Reveal the special strengths You've given my child. Help me to offer pertinent suggestions and then to step back and let him run with You. Remind him that all blessings are from You and that You have good plans for his future.

Help me to show my son in concrete, tangible ways that I love him solely for who he is and not what he does. More importantly, so do You.

Amen.

Every step toward Christ kills a doubt.

Theodore Ledyard Cuyler

# When my child is growing in faith . . .

*[Jesus said] If you have faith as small as a mustard seed, you can say to this mountain, 'Move from here to there' and it will move. Nothing will be impossible for you.*
MATTHEW 17:20

*Let your roots grow down into him and draw up nourishment from him, so you will grow in faith, strong and vigorous in the truth you were taught.*
COLOSSIANS 2:7 NLT

*I will continue with you so that you will grow and experience the joy of your faith.*
PHILIPPIANS 1:25 NLT

*I long to visit you so that I can impart to you the faith that will help your church grow strong in the Lord. . . . I want not only to share my faith with you but to be encouraged by yours: Each of us will be a blessing to the other.*
ROMANS 1:11-12 TLB

# . . . I will pray.

Gracious Redeemer,

I can scarcely contain my excitement over my child's freshly acquired taste for spiritual things and hunger for Your Word. She rapidly fires questions at me, thirsty and spongelike, soaking up Your truth and Your answers.

I pray that her faith will grow strong as she partakes of Your Word. May she be encouraged as You answer her prayers according to Your faithfulness. I ask You to provide Bible studies and youth activities to feed the fire that has been kindled within her. When the excitement wanes, as it sometimes does, I pray that the habits of prayer and fellowship with believers will be deeply ingrained in her character.

Lead and anoint her youth sponsors and Sunday school teachers. Help them prepare lessons that are relevant, fresh, and exciting.

I pray that my child will learn how to use Your Word as the lamp for her feet. Help her to hide it in her heart so that she won't fall into the trap of sin. May Your commands become so ingrained in her that her walk of faith is as natural as breathing.

Thank You for the gift of watching her faith grow.

Amen.

Belief is truth held in the mind;
faith is fire in the heart.

Joseph Fort Newton

# When my child needs to forgive . . .

*Smart people know how to hold their tongue;*
*their grandeur is to forgive and forget.*
Proverbs 19:11 msg

❀

*[ Jesus said] In prayer there is a connection between what*
*God does and what you do. You can't get forgiveness from*
*God, for instance, without also forgiving others. If you refuse*
*to do your part, you cut yourself off from God's part.*
Matthew 6:14-15 msg

❀

*Be kind and loving to each other,*
*and forgive each other just as God*
*forgave you in Christ.*
Ephesians 4:32 ncv

❀

*[ Jesus said] Do not judge, and you will not be judged;*
*and do not condemn, and you will not be condemned;*
*pardon, and you will be pardoned.*
Luke 6:37 nasb

# . . . I will pray.

Precious Protector,

Today my child learned the hard lesson that not everyone can be trusted. He experienced that dreadful feeling of betrayal that happens when you've entrusted another person with your secrets, your dreams, your fears, and then those things get back to you via someone else. He is hurt, angry, bewildered, and disillusioned. I'm furious right along with him. How dare someone hurt my child!

How easily the instinct rises to return the "favor" in kind. Instead, help me to empathize with my child, to mourn the loss of that particular brand of innocence, and then to teach him a better way—Yours.

I ask You to lend both of us the strength of character to forgive, to pray for our enemies (even this child who betrayed my son's confidence), and to show them Your kindness. Don't let the seeds of bitterness or revenge take root in my son. Let me teach him the art of gentle power, using experience to gain wisdom, but not as an excuse to refuse to trust again.

Thank You for going first, for forgiving enemies of a far greater magnitude from the agony of the cross.

Amen.

As we practice the work of forgiveness
we discover more and more
that forgiveness and healing are one.

Agnes Sanford

# When my child needs good friends . . .

*As iron sharpens iron, a friend sharpens a friend.*
PROVERBS 27:17 NLT

*There is a friend who sticks closer than a brother.*
PROVERBS 18:24 NASB

*Friends love through all kinds of weather.*
PROVERBS 17:17 MSG

*Two are better than one, because they have a good reward for
their toil. For if they fall, one will lift up the other.*
ECCLESIASTES 4:9-10 NRSV

*Your friendship was a miracle-wonder,
love far exceeding anything I've known—
or ever hope to know.*
2 SAMUEL 1:26 MSG

# . . . I will pray.

Friend and Father,

My child has plenty of playmates, a passel of acquaintances, and a bevy of classmates, but no special friends. Bosom buddies. Soul mates. Those with like hearts.

God, friendships are so important all through life. But in these, my child's formative years, I pray that You would lead her into the right kinds of friendships.

Friends have such a powerful impact on our lives—affecting our character, our happiness, even what we do for entertainment. Doubtless Jesus spent much time in prayer before choosing those twelve who would be His closest friends, His disciples.

For my child I pray for the gift of special friends. Not just people to do things with or share lockers with, but true friends. I want for her the type of friendship shared by Jonathan and David in the Bible—friends who will challenge her, inspire her, stretch her faith, and point her toward You, friends with whom she can giggle, bake cookies, trade notes, and confide.

Because I know You love my child even more than I do, I trust You to provide these friends for her in Your perfect timing. Thank You for being our very best Friend.

Amen.

A friend is one who knows you as you are,
understands where you've been, accepts who you've
become, and still, gently invites you to grow.

Author Unknown

# When my child needs to discover his or her gifts . . .

*Just as our bodies have many parts and each part has a special function, so it is with Christ's body. We are all parts of his one body, and each of us has different work to do. And since we are all one body in Christ, we belong to each other, and each of us needs all the others. God has given each of us the ability to do certain things well. If your gift is that of serving others, serve them well. If you are a teacher, do a good job of teaching.  If your gift is to encourage others, do it! If you have money, share it generously. If God has given you leadership ability, take the responsibility seriously. And if you have a gift for showing kindness to others, do it gladly.*

ROMANS 12:4-8 NLT

*God's various gifts are handed out everywhere; but they all originate in God's Spirit. God's various ministries are carried out everywhere; but they all originate in God's Spirit. God's various expressions of power are in action everywhere; but God himself is behind it all. Each person is given something to do that shows who God is: Everyone gets in on it, everyone benefits. All kinds of things are handed out by the Spirit, and to all kinds of people! . . . All these gifts have a common origin, but are handed out one by one by the one Spirit of God. He decides who gets what, and when.*

1 CORINTHIANS 12:4-7,11 MSG

# . . . I will pray.

Holy God,

My child is dabbling in every conceivable instrument, sport, club, and gathering, yet she hasn't found her niche. You create each of us with certain gifts that we can develop and use to serve You. Give me keen discernment as I seek to discover that hidden treasure in my child. Guide us to specific activities that will be the best match for her. Help us then to nurture the budding ability.

As with the development of any talent, it will likely become progressively more difficult. Boredom or discouragement might set in. I pray that at those times my child will learn the value of discipline and perseverance, that she will realize that nothing worthwhile can be developed without some effort.

Father, I also ask that she would take a healthy pride, but never arrogance, in this gift with which You've blessed her. That she would delight in the wonder and power of being able to do something uniquely well and that she will make it a praise offering to You.

Thank You for the astounding variety of canvases on which we can paint our contribution to the world and Your kingdom. You are worthy of our praise.

Amen.

Your talent is God's gift to you.
What you do with it is your gift back to God.
Leo Buscaglia

# When my child needs to learn to express gratitude . . .

*Accept my grateful thanks and teach me your desires.*
PSALM 119:108 TLB

✿

*Oh, how grateful and thankful I am to the Lord because he is so good. I will sing praise to the name of the Lord who is above all lords.*
PSALM 7:17 TLB

✿

*Do not be proud; be humble and grateful.*
ROMANS 11:20 TLB

✿

*If I'm sleepless at midnight,
I spend the hours in grateful reflection.*
PSALM 63:6 MSG

✿

*I am grateful to God—whom I worship with a clear conscience.*
2 TIMOTHY 1:3 NRSV

# . . . I will pray.

Loving Father,

I was so exasperated this afternoon! And I have a confession to make—I hate making trips to the grocery store with all the children. They morph into miniature tornadoes of greed the moment supercenter doors open.

The rampant materialism that is so prevalent in the world constantly seeks to undermine our ability to enjoy the things we already possess. Help us to recognize when it raises its ugly head, and remind all of us to develop an attitude of gratitude. Help us replace the spirit of "gimmee" with a heart that expresses thanks, a heart that is moved with compassion to give to others.

God, I do want my children to have the good life, and I know You want that for us, but I don't want our lives to be out of balance. Give me wisdom as I make the decisions about what my children can and cannot have. Help me to set a good example before them and not give in to my own tendency to be greedy.

We have so much to be thankful for, Father, and for that, I give You praise.

Amen.

Cultivate the thankful Spirit!
It will be to you a perpetual feast.

John R. MacDuff

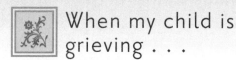

# When my child is grieving . . .

*[The Lord] was despised and rejected by men;*
*a man of sorrows, and acquainted with grief. . . .*
*Surely he has borne our griefs*
*and carried our sorrows.*

ISAIAH 53:3-4 RSV

*[Jesus said] Truly, truly, I say to you, that you will weep and*
*lament, but the world will rejoice; you will grieve, but your*
*grief will be turned into joy.*

JOHN 16:20 NASB

*I say, "It is my grief*
*that the right hand of the Most High has changed."*
*I will call to mind the deeds of the LORD;*
*yea, I will remember thy wonders of old.*
*I will meditate on all thy work,*
*and muse on thy mighty deeds.*

PSALM 77:10-12 RSV

✿

*The LORD is near to the brokenhearted*
*And saves those who are crushed in spirit.*

PSALM 34:18 NASB

# . . . I will pray.

Comforting Father,

Today I stood next to my child and held him as he cried. Father, loss is always hard and this one was especially so.

I understand that loss was not a part of Your original plan, but it has dogged mankind since the fall of man. Funerals. Lives cut short. Friends who move away. Breakups. Betrayals. Even the loss of trust or innocence.

Allow my child the clarity to see that through every loss, every heartache, there is one constant: You are forever there. You are the same yesterday, today, and forever. Thank You for caring so deeply about our hurts.

Remind us that no matter the loss, we don't have to grieve as those who have no hope, because for us, this life is not all there is. One day heartaches and good-byes will vanish from our vocabularies.

Help me to use this situation to teach my child about Your faithfulness, for I know that over time there will be losses greater than this. But in the midst of them all, You will be there and joy will spring forth once again.

Amen.

God is closest to those whose hearts are broken.

Jewish Proverb

# When my child needs guidance . . .

*The LORD will guide you continually.*
ISAIAH 58:11 RSV

*I am always with you;*
*you have held my hand.*
*You guide me with your advice.*
PSALM 73:23-24 NCV

*[Zechariah said] Heaven's dawn is about to break upon us,*
*to give light to those who sit in darkness and . . .*
*to guide us to the path of peace.*
LUKE 1:78-79 TLB

*Your ears will hear a word behind you,*
*"This is the way, walk in it."*
ISAIAH 30:21 NASB

*This God . . . will be our guide even to the end.*
PSALM 48:14

# . . . I will pray.

Father God,

I'm discovering that one of the most difficult things about this craft called motherhood is the letting-go part. I was great at rocking my child as an infant, holding his hand as he started to walk, and being the room mother every chance I got. But now I need to relinquish him into Your capable, kind hands in an ever-greater way.

I pray that You will guide my child to the right classes and teachers. I pray that they might be people of faith, or that he can be salt and light for them. Guide his study so that he learns the value of work and discipline and that his mind can clearly recall information.

Lead my child to friends who will encourage him to fulfill his potential, and guide us as we plan ahead for his career. Grant him wisdom and discernment beyond his years as we seek to honestly evaluate his strengths, interests, talents, and weaknesses.

Work through me to lend him sound advice, experience, and encouragement. Grant him assurance of Your great love and confidence that as long as he includes You in his plans, he will be truly successful.

Amen.

Abraham did not know the way,
but he knew the Guide.

Lee Roberson

# When my child is
# overcoming a bad habit . . .

*Sin shall not have dominion over you,*
*for you are not under law but under grace.*
ROMANS 6:14 NKJV

*In all these things we are more than conquerors*
*through him who loved us.*
ROMANS 8:37 RSV

*Thanks be to God, who always leads us*
*in triumph in Christ.*
2 CORINTHIANS 2:14 NASB

*Be glad, good people! Fly to GOD!*
*Good-hearted people, make praise your habit.*
PSALM 64:10 MSG

❀

*[Cornelius] was a thoroughly good man. He had led everyone*
*in his house to live worshipfully before God, was always*
*helping people in need, and had the habit of prayer.*
ACTS 10:2 MSG

# . . . I will pray.

Gracious God,

I'm at the end of my rope. It seems like such a silly thing, but when I look at my child's bad habit, I am aggravated and impatient. From my perspective, it doesn't seem as if she's trying. I've explained about being responsible and nagged about the value of discipline, but she just shrugs her shoulders. "It's a habit, I guess, Mom."

In the big scheme of things, I know this isn't the most important, Father, but I do want her to learn self-control. Little bad habits can so quickly lead to bigger ones.

Help me to turn the spotlight on myself and my own habits that might need to be broken. Help me to blend empathy and compassion with firmness and creative motivation.

Thank You that because we belong to You, we are more than conquerors and can overcome the world—even our bad habits. Let me teach her that You care and will help us in all things, no matter how big or small. Help her to focus on the rewards of living a fruitful, disciplined life.

Thank You for knowing what we need before we ask.

Amen.

When we have practiced good actions awhile,
they become easy; when they are easy, we take
pleasure in them; when they please us, we do them
frequently; and then, by frequency of act,
they grow into a habit.

John Tillotson

# When my child needs emotional healing . . .

*Floods of sorrow pour upon me like a thundering cataract.*
*Yet day by day the Lord also pours out his steadfast love*
*upon me, and through the night I sing his songs and*
*pray to God who gives me life.*
PSALM 42:7-8 TLB

*He heals the brokenhearted and binds up their wounds.*
PSALM 147:3 NKJV

*My health fails; my spirits droop, yet God remains!*
*He is the strength of my heart; he is mine forever!*
PSALM 73:26 TLB

*I will never lay aside your laws,*
*for you have used them to restore my joy and health.*
PSALM 119:93 TLB

*Some people like to make cutting remarks,*
*but the words of the wise soothe and heal.*
PROVERBS 12:18 TLB

# . . . I will pray.

Worthy Creator,

Seeing my child struggle is so hard. Emotions are such fragile things. A cross word, a rejection, a critical comment on a paper—all of these, and so much more, can cause such stress on her ever-growing, ever-changing feelings. Children can encapsulate one moment, one stray word, and stretch it over their entire world, for good or for bad.

Right now my child is struggling. She wonders if her work will measure up. She is questioning her judgment, her choices, even her worth. Show her that experience can be a wise and useful—although sometimes painful—teacher.

Father, give me wise words, open arms, and a spirit of receptivity. Nudge me to be available when I need to talk to her or just listen. Help me forgive anyone who causes hurt to my child's spirit.

Help me to be gently encouraging, consistently affirming, and ever loving, without ever being saccharine. Children are so perceptive. Help me direct her to what she needs the most—You.

Just now she needs to be flooded with Your grace, drenched in Your peace, bathed in Your love, soaked in Your compassion, and held in Your arms. Let it rain.

Amen.

Apt words have power to assuage
The tumors of a troubled mind
And are as balm to fester'd wounds.

John Milton

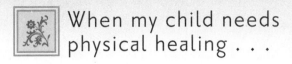 When my child needs
physical healing . . .

*Keep these thoughts ever in mind; let them penetrate deep*
*within your heart, for they will mean real life for you,*
*and radiant health.*

PROVERBS 4:21-22 TLB

*He himself bore our sins in his body on the tree,*
*that we might die to sin and live to righteousness.*
*By his wounds you have been healed.*

1 PETER 2:24 RSV

*[The Lord says] For you who honor me, goodness will shine*
*on you like the sun, with healing in its rays.*

MALACHI 4:2 NCV

🌼

*No doubt you know that God anointed Jesus of Nazareth*
*with the Holy Spirit and with power. Then Jesus went*
*around doing good and healing all who were oppressed by the*
*Devil, for God was with him.*

ACTS 10:38 NLT

# . . . I will pray.

Father God,

I sit here in the hospital, running my fingers over my child's jacket. The staff just took him for some tests, and here I sit, alone. How I treasure my son. Thank You for such a gift.

God, You have a Son too. You understand my fears—my not wanting him to experience any pain. Yet this situation is different. I realize that at some point every child has something: an illness, a surgery, some stitches, the need for antibiotics. But Your Son died for our sins.

Despite the stark contrasts, I know You understand a mother's heart. Guide the skillful hands of the doctors who will diagnose him; work through the nurses who will oversee his care. I pray that any medicine will be effective and that You will protect him from negative side effects.

I ask You to please watch over every aspect of my child's treatment. Encamp Your angels around him. Be with me while I wait. Help me to focus on Your sovereignty and to feel Your peace. Hold my son as surely as I am holding his coat.

By His stripes we are healed. Thank You for being our Great Physician.

Amen.

## I treated him, God cured him.

Ambroise Paré

# When my child is dealing with difficulties at home . . .

*How very good and pleasant it is*
*when kindred live together in unity!*
*. . . For there the LORD ordained his blessing,*
*life forevermore.*

PSALM 133:1,3 NRSV

*Rejoice with those who rejoice, weep with those who weep.*
*Live in harmony with one another; do not be haughty.*

ROMANS 12:15-16 RSV

❁

*Above all these put on love, which binds everything*
*together in perfect harmony.*

COLOSSIANS 3:14 RSV

❁

*All of you, have unity of spirit, sympathy, love for one*
*another, a tender heart, and a humble mind.*

1 PETER 3:8 NRSV

❁

*Finally, brethren, rejoice, be made complete, be comforted,*
*be like-minded, live in peace; and the God of love*
*and peace will be with you.*

2 CORINTHIANS 13:11 NASB

# . . . I will pray.

Maker of Families,

I know You never intended for home to be anything but a refuge—a safe place in the night, a warm place in the cold, a dry place in the rain, a celebration place for our joys, and a soft landing pad for our hurts.

Unfortunately, ours doesn't resemble this right now, and it's affecting my child. A variety of circumstances are putting pressure on us, and we all seem to be on edge. I snap at the slightest requests and am impatient with everyone. And we're so busy hurtling from one activity to another that we've forgotten how to be a family. To be still. To simply be.

As a parent, I know it's my job to help fix this, but I can't do it without Your help. Order our priorities. Guide our days. Open our hearts to more fully hear You. Don't let us fill our days with so many activities that we are merely "doing life." Instead, let us embrace life with delight.

We invite You to sit with us tonight, an honored Guest at our table. Thank You for the privilege of family. Thank You for being the Head of our home.

Amen.

It is [at home]—with fellow family members—
we hammer out our convictions on the anvil of
relationships. It is there we cultivate the valuable
things in life, like attitudes, memories, beliefs, and
most of all, character.

Charles R. Swindoll

# When my child needs a renewal of hope . . .

*Glory be to God! By his mighty power at work within us,*
*he is able to accomplish infinitely more than we would*
*ever dare to ask or hope.*

EPHESIANS 3:20 NLT

*[The Scriptures] give us hope and encouragement*
*as we wait patiently for God's promises.*

ROMANS 15:4 NLT

*May the God of hope fill you with all joy and*
*peace in believing, so that by the power of the*
*Holy Spirit you may abound in hope.*

ROMANS 15:13 RSV

*Why are you down in the dumps, dear soul?*
*Why are you crying the blues?*
*Fix my eyes on God—*
*soon I'll be praising again.*
*He puts a smile on my face.*
*He's my God.*

PSALM 43:5 MSG

# . . . I will pray.

Author of Hope,

My child usually soars like a kite in a playful March wind. Now it's as though her tail has been wound through trees, ripped ragged by rigid branches, and strung so tightly it might snap. And because I love her, my emotions are bound up tightly with hers. I soar when she soars and plummet along with her.

I ache to see her so discouraged, and it seems difficult to offer adequate help when I battle highs and lows of my own. Please remind us that no matter how hopeless a situation seems, we are never alone, we are never without hope. I am grateful that You have promised never to leave us. Thank You that Your mercies are new every morning.

Show us by the way You care for Your creation that we are so much more valuable to You than tiny sparrows and regal roses. Help us remember that each day is a fresh start, a second chance full of opportunities and the possibility of adventure, wrapped with hope.

Hope is Your best gift, outside of Jesus Christ. Thank You. Amen.

O hope! Dazzling, radiant hope!
What a change thou bringest to the hopeless;
brightening the darkened paths,
and cheering the lonely way.

Aimee Semple McPherson

# When my child is touched by injustice . . .

*Do not repay anyone evil for evil. Be careful to do what is right in the eyes of everybody. If it is possible, as far as it depends on you, live at peace with everyone. Do not take revenge, my friends, but leave room for God's wrath, for it is written: "It is mine to avenge; I will repay," says the Lord. On the contrary: "If your enemy is hungry, feed him; if he is thirsty, give him something to drink. In doing this, you will heap burning coals on his head." Do not be overcome by evil, but overcome evil with good.*
ROMANS 12:17-21

*The LORD your God is going with you! He will fight for you against your enemies, and he will give you victory!*
DEUTERONOMY 20:4 NLT

*The LORD will vindicate his people and have compassion on his servants.*
PSALM 135:14

*Many evils confront the [consistently] righteous, but the Lord delivers him out of them all.*
PSALM 34:19 AMP

# . . . I will pray.

Dear Lord,

It hurts when my child is the target of injustice. I often tell him to simply ignore the problem. But that doesn't take away the pain in his heart.

It would be different, Father, if my child were causing part of the problem. At least then there would be a reason for the hatred and meanness being directed toward him. But how do I answer "What did I do, Mom?" or "Why me?" when the cruelty is inflicted just to be mean?

Help me, Lord, to simply be there for my child when the hurts of this world become a heavy burden. Help me to teach him to turn to Your Son, the One who knows just how it feels to suffer injustice at the hands of others.

But most of all, Father, let me be able to teach him to bear his burdens with a smile, to respond in love as Jesus did. Things aren't always fair, but my child can be a lifter of others' burdens in a world full of injustice. I ask You to show him that although life can be unfair, it is also wonderful.

Thank You for always being fair, Father.

Amen.

There is no greater opportunity to influence our fellowman for Christ than to respond with love when we have been unmistakably wronged. Then the difference between Christian love and the values of the world are most brilliantly evident.

James C. Dobson

# When my child is feeling insecure . . .

*The LORD is exalted, for he dwells on high . . .*
*and he will be the stability of your times,*
*abundance of salvation, wisdom, and knowledge.*
ISAIAH 33:5-6 RSV

*He who dwells in the secret place of the Most High shall*
*remain stable and fixed under the shadow of the Almighty*
*[Whose power no foe can withstand].*
PSALM 91:1 AMP

*The LORD is my rock and my fortress and my deliverer;*
*My God, my strength, in whom I will trust;*
*My shield and the horn of my salvation, my stronghold.*
PSALM 18:2 NKJV

❁

*[The righteous] are not afraid of evil tidings;*
*their hearts are firm, secure in the Lord.*
PSALM 112:7 NRSV

# . . . I will pray.

Lord God,

It seems like only yesterday I gave birth to my child. Life was so much simpler then. I was the center of her universe, and cradled in my arms she was warm and secure. But each stage of growth has provided opportunities to shake that security. No longer can I shield her from everything that would cause her pain or discomfort.

The troubled look on her face tells me she is feeling insecure. I want to rush in and make everything okay, but I realize this is just another step in the growing-up process. Another step toward maturity.

While I can lend an open ear, a shoulder to cry on, You are the only true Source of security. As I point her to You and assure her that she can find the stability she needs in You, I ask You to fill her with confidence—confidence in Your love for her, confidence in the lovely girl You've created her to be, confidence in the gifts with which You have graced her.

Someday I will leave this earth for heaven, but You will remain the secure Rock on which she can stand. Amen.

In God's faithfulness lies eternal security.

Corrie ten Boom

# When my child needs joy and happiness . . .

LORD, *you have made me happy by what you have done;*
*I will sing for joy about what your hands have done.*
PSALM 92:4 NCV

*You have made known to me the path of life;*
*you will fill me with joy in your presence,*
*with eternal pleasures at your right hand.*
PSALM 16:11

*Taste and see that the LORD is good.*
*Oh, the joys of those who trust in him!*
PSALM 34:8 NLT

*The joy of the Lord is your strength.*
*You must not be dejected and sad!*
NEHEMIAH 8:10 TLB

# . . . I will pray.

Dear Father,

What am I to do when my child thinks it's all about him? No matter how much he gets or how much he does, it is never enough. Jealousy over what others have or are able to do makes him mad. What do I do when he refuses to let go of the situation and it ruins everything? How can one child enjoy being so miserable?

Father, I cannot seem to make him see that joy and happiness come from within, that true joy is based on You—not on outward circumstances—and that he creates his own unhappiness. Is it because I do the same thing? Does he see joy in me, Father, no matter how hectic life is around me? Or am I cranky and upset when life doesn't go my way?

Help me to be truly happy, Lord. Let my joy be in You. Make my happiness overflow, even on the rough days, so that my child sees You. Let him see that we decide whether we will be joyful or not. That things and situations are always going to change as we go through life, but You never change.

Thank You for being the unchanging Source of joy for me and for my child, Lord. Amen.

Happiness is the spiritual experience of living every minute with love, grace, and gratitude.

Denis Waitley

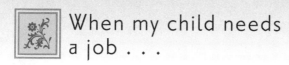

# When my child needs a job . . .

*You will eat the fruit of your labor;*
*blessings and prosperity will be yours.*
PSALM 128:2

*That every man who eats and drinks sees good in all his*
*labor—it is the gift of God.*
ECCLESIASTES 3:13 NASB

❖

*It is good and fitting for one to eat and drink, and to enjoy*
*the good of all his labor in which he toils under the sun all*
*the days of his life which God gives him; for it is his heritage.*
*As for every man to whom God has given riches and wealth,*
*and given him power to eat of it, to receive his heritage and*
*rejoice in his labor—this is the gift of God.*
ECCLESIASTES 5:18-19 NKJV

❖

*Let the thief no longer steal, but rather let him labor,*
*doing honest work with his hands, so that he may be able*
*to give to those in need.*
EPHESIANS 4:28 RSV

# . . . I will pray.

Dear Lord,

My son lost his chance at a good job today. It was a real blow to him, Father. We spent the afternoon trying to sort out his feelings of inadequacy and hopelessness. I remember when I went through this very same thing, Lord. It was hard to trust that things would turn out all right eventually.

Lord, lift him up and bring peace to his heart. Help us to be an encouragement to him. Guide his path and provide employment for him. He just wants to take care of his needs. Father, You are the Provider of all good things. Let him trust in You for the future and for a job.

This could be a good thing, Lord—a time for him to stretch and grow. Maybe even find a job that will suit him better. As I bring him before You in prayer, I am resting in the knowledge that You know all of our needs. I ask that You would show him how to rely fully on You. You never fail.

Thank You for being the Giver of all things.

Amen.

Each individual has his own kind of living
assigned to him by the Lord as a sort of sentry post.

John Calvin

# When my child is lacking in kindness and compassion . . .

Chosen by God for this new life of love, dress in the wardrobe
God picked out for you: compassion, kindness,
humility, quiet strength, discipline.

COLOSSIANS 3:12 MSG

All of you be of one mind, having compassion for one
another; love as brothers, be tenderhearted, be courteous;
not returning evil for evil or reviling for reviling,
but on the contrary blessing.

1 PETER 3:8-9 NKJV

❖

[Jesus said] Try to show as much compassion as your Father
does. Never criticize or condemn—or it will all come back on
you. Go easy on others; then they will do the same for you.

LUKE 6:36-37 TLB

# . . . I will pray.

Dear Father,

Here I sit praying for my child again. I think my greatest frustration comes from trying to make her see how her lack of kindness and compassion hurts others, to truly make her understand the damage she does to friends and family when she lashes out at them. Lord, we cannot expect others to treat us with compassion if we have none ourselves. I want her to know that, Father.

Lord, help me to teach her to empathize with others, to be able to put herself in their shoes and treat them the way she would want to be treated. That's going to be a stretch for her right now, but I know You can reach her on a level that I cannot.

I ask, too, that You would help me to be a better example, showing compassion and kindness not only to those I'm close to but also to strangers who have no way to repay my kindness.

I'm placing my child in Your capable hands, Lord. Be merciful to her, I pray, and show me how to teach her a better way of living.

Amen.

The heart benevolent and kind
The most resembles God.

Robert Burns

# When my child is learning to manage money . . .

[ Jesus said] Whoever can be trusted with very little can also
be trusted with much, and whoever is dishonest with very
little will also be dishonest with much.

LUKE 16:10

The wise have wealth and luxury,
but fools spend whatever they get.

PROVERBS 21:20 NLT

Go to the ant . . .
consider its ways, and be wise.
Without having any chief
or officer or ruler,
it prepares its food in summer,
and gathers its sustenance in harvest.

PROVERBS 6:6-8 NRSV

She looks over a field and buys it,
then, with money she's put aside, plants a garden.

PROVERBS 31:16 MSG

# . . . I will pray.

Dear Heavenly Father,

Our son got his first paycheck today. He wants to be financially responsible, and I'm sensing it's time for me to let him learn to be just that. My first impulse, of course, is to micromanage every spending choice for him, but I know that won't teach him anything and will actually handicap him in the future.

Part of the problem, Lord, is that I question whether my example in the area of finances has been a good one. How many times have I splurged and spent more than my budget allowed? Learning to spend wisely is not easy. Letting him make wrong choices is painful. But, Lord, I don't want my poor choices to cause him to go down the same frustrating path.

Give me strength, Lord, to let go and let You work with my child in the area of financial responsibility. Show me how to provide proper guidance and to be strong when he messes up, allowing him to make mistakes and learn from them.

Thank You for loving us and caring about every part of our lives.

Amen.

To get money is difficult, to keep it more difficult,
but to spend it wisely most difficult of all.

Author Unknown

# When my child has been rejected . . .

*[The Lord said] You are My servant,*
*I have chosen you and not rejected you.*
ISAIAH 41:9 NASB

*[Jesus said] The one who rejects you rejects Me;*
*and he who rejects Me rejects the One who sent Me.*
LUKE 10:16 NASB

*He hath made us accepted in the beloved.*
EPHESIANS 1:6 KJV

*[Jesus said] Those the Father has given me will come to me,*
*and I will never reject them.*
JOHN 6:37 NLT

*Even if my father and mother abandon me,*
*the LORD will hold me close.*
PSALM 27:10 NLT

# . . . I will pray.

Loving Father,

Rejection is tough, and my child is struggling. She's such a great person, and it seems so unfair that certain other people can't see that. Help me to be a source of encouragement and self-esteem for her.

Lord, You and I know that rejection isn't always personal, but she sure isn't ready to hear that right now. Help her to understand that being accepted isn't what's important, but it's doing her best, keeping her chin up, and seeing things through that makes the difference.

Allow me, Father, to show her Your unconditional love through my love for her. She needs to know You will never turn her away. I want to be able to encourage her to try again and understand that most rejections are temporary. Being rejected, after all, is a chance to become better, to learn, to grow, to get tougher. I thank You, Father, that there is no threat of rejection from You. No matter how we mess up and come short of doing our best, You love and accept us completely.

Amen.

You don't have to be alone in your hurt! Comfort is yours . . . And it's all been made possible by your Savior. . . . He willingly chose isolation so that you might never be alone in your hurt and sorrow.

Joni Eareckson Tada

# When my child is not in relationship with God . . .

*I have no greater joy than this,*
*to hear of my children walking in the truth.*
3 JOHN 1:4 NASB

*If we are faithless, He remains faithful,*
*for He cannot deny Himself.*
2 TIMOTHY 2:13 NASB

*[Jesus said] Plead with the Lord of the harvest*
*to send out more laborers to help you, for the harvest is so*
*plentiful and the workers so few.*
LUKE 10:2 TLB

*[Jesus said] And I, as I am lifted up from the earth,*
*will attract everyone to me and gather them around me.*
JOHN 12:32 MSG

*[Jesus said] Behold, I stand at the door and knock;*
*if any one hears my voice and opens the door,*
*I will come in to him and eat with him, and he with me.*
REVELATION 3:20 RSV

# . . . I will pray.

Dear Lord,

My heart is breaking, Father. I brought my child up to love You, and I know at one time she did. When she was a child, church was her favorite place to be no matter how often we went. But it's not that way now. These days she wants nothing to do with You. How can this be? How can she turn her back on You?

Lord, Your Word says if we teach our children the right way to go that when they are grown they will not stray from that teaching. Oh, I am clinging to that hope, Father! All I can see for her future is a life full of loneliness and separation from You. That is not what I want for her.

Thank You that You keep Your Word, Lord. I know You will be waiting for her when she decides to come back. Help me rest in the knowledge that although she seems to have forgotten You, You will never forget her, never ever leave her side. You will carry her in Your arms when she doesn't even know You are there.

Thank You for loving her even more than I do.

Amen.

Our task is to live our personal communion with Christ with such intensity as to make it contagious.

Paul Tournier

# When my child is sad . . .

I am sad and hurting.
God, save me and protect me.
. . . The LORD listens to those in need
and does not look down on captives.
PSALM 69:29,33 NCV

Why am I so sad?
Why am I so upset?
I should put my hope in God
and keep praising him,
my Savior and my God.
PSALM 42:11 NCV

You changed my sorrow into dancing.
You took away my clothes of sadness,
and clothed me in happiness.
PSALM 30:11 NCV

# . . . I will pray.

Dear God,

All of us were affected by this loss—suddenly an irreplaceable part of our lives was no more. My child has had an especially hard time dealing with her feelings about the situation. She doesn't seem to know what to do with all the sadness.

How do I teach her that sadness is part of life? Without it there would be no true joy. One day, Father, You promise to wipe away all our tears, gather us to Yourself, and move us into those homes You've prepared for us in heaven. But until that day comes, we need to know how to deal with broken hearts.

As I dry the tears on her face, Lord, dry the tears in her heart. Help her appreciate the years of joy that came before. Those years make the loss seem much greater now. Still the sadness can't diminish what for so long was so wonderful.

Thank You, God, that You allow us to experience storms so that we are able to truly enjoy the sunshine. Thank You for being able to make a broken heart whole again. Please whisk away the clouds of sadness in my child's life.

Amen.

Christ can do wonders with a broken heart
if given all the pieces.
Proverb

# When my child needs salvation . . .

*The god of this age has blinded the minds of unbelievers,
so that they cannot see the light of the gospel of the glory of
Christ, who is the image of God.*
2 CORINTHIANS 4:4

*Go out into the world uncorrupted, a breath of fresh air
in this squalid and polluted society. Provide people with
a glimpse of good living and of the living God.
Carry the light-giving Message into the night.*
PHILIPPIANS 2:15-16 MSG

*Everyone who calls on the name of the Lord shall be saved.*
ROMANS 10:13 NRSV

*[Jesus said] God so loved the world that he gave his one and
only Son, that whoever believes in him shall not perish
but have eternal life.*
JOHN 3:16

*God our Savior . . . desires all men to be saved and
to come to the knowledge of the truth.*
1 TIMOTHY 2:3-4 NASB

# . . . I will pray.

Merciful Lord,

I bring my son to You today, Lord. He needs You in his life. He has to realize how wrong the path is that he is on and what a mistake it is to shut You out. He is struggling with this, Father. He knows what he should do, but the barrier seems too great to cross. I know how he feels; I have built a few of those barriers myself.

I pray, Lord, that You would break down those walls. Help him to see his need for salvation and Your guidance. Draw him to Yourself. Reveal to Him how good You are. I know You won't give up on him, Lord! Prepare his heart even now for the next time he hears Your Word, that he might be receptive to Your call to "Follow Me."

Thank You, Lord, for my own salvation. What a wonderful thing it is to be forgiven and have a home waiting in heaven. Thank You that You never gave up on me. Surely there must have been days You wanted to! But the loving Father You are will keep gently urging my child's heart toward Yours. Thank You, Father.

Amen.

❁

God has his own secret stairway into every heart.

Author Unknown

# When my child is struggling in school . . .

*I have more understanding than all my teachers,*
*For Your testimonies are my meditation.*
PSALM 119:99 NKJV

*These are the wise words of Solomon son of David,*
*king of Israel.. . . Make the uneducated smarter and*
*give knowledge and sense to the young.*
PROVERBS 1:1,4 NCV

*[ Jesus said] The Helper, the Holy Spirit, whom the Father*
*will send in My name, He will teach you all things, and*
*bring to your remembrance all that I said to you.*
JOHN 14:26 NASB

*[ Jesus said] When the Father sends the Comforter*
*instead of me—and by the Comforter I mean the*
*Holy Spirit—he will teach you much, as well as*
*remind you of everything I myself have told you.*
JOHN 14:26 TLB

# . . . I will pray.

Dear Jesus,

I am beginning to hate school as much as my daughter does! I'm convinced that neither one of us will make it through this year without Your help. O Lord, help my child conquer this situation at school.

It isn't that she doesn't work hard, Lord. She seems to be doing everything right—except maybe getting those assignments in on time. Sometimes they seem to disappear into her book bag never to be seen again. It's difficult to know if she's dodging or she just doesn't get it.

Give me wisdom, Lord, to deal with this situation here at home. I know how important her education is. I ask also for wisdom for her teachers. Give them the ability to see below the surface and identify the root causes of her struggles. Most of all, I pray for her. I know how difficult it can be to hang in there when nothing seems to make sense. I don't want her to be discouraged. Her best is all I can ask of her. Give her the ability to persevere and stick to her studies.

I thank You, Lord, that our best is all You ask of us. And even when we do less than that You love us anyway.

Amen.

Education is not the filling of a pail,
but the lighting of a fire.

William Butler Yeats

# When my child needs self-control . . .

*The fruit of the Spirit is . . . self-control.*
GALATIANS 5:22-23

*Since we belong to the day, let us be self-controlled, putting on faith and love as a breastplate.*
1 THESSALONIANS 5:8

*The grace of God that brings salvation has appeared to all men. It teaches us to say "No" to ungodliness and worldly passions, and to live self-controlled, upright and godly lives.*
TITUS 2:11-12

*The wise words of Solomon . . .
will teach you how to be wise and self-controlled.*
PROVERBS 1:1,3 NCV

*Watch your words and hold your tongue;
you'll save yourself a lot of grief.*
PROVERBS 21:23 MSG

# . . . I will pray.

Dear Father,

I lost it again today. I have no idea how I expect to teach my child to control herself when I can't. The disagreement escalated into a shouting match. One little incident and she loses her cool. It seems as if none of us can even look at her without causing a problem.

First, I ask You to forgive my own out-of-control behavior. I need to walk away and seek Your face when things begin to get heated. As for my child, I ask that You will help her to take a deep breath before reacting. She needs to learn to calm down and think first. Maybe, Lord, I need to take her by the hand and then kneel with her in prayer before I even attempt to talk to her. My failure to be calm has surely bled over onto her.

I want to teach my child to look to You when her feelings are overflowing, Lord, and not to let emotions rule her thoughts and actions. We can both handle things in a smoother, calmer fashion if we depend on You. Thank You, Lord, that no matter how fast things are spinning, You hold everything securely in Your hands.

Amen.

Self-control is the ability to keep cool
while someone is making it hot for you.
Author Unknown

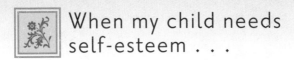

# When my child needs self-esteem . . .

*We are his workmanship, created in Christ Jesus.*
EPHESIANS 2:10 RSV

❧

*God created people in his own image.*
GENESIS 1:27 NLT

❧

*[Jesus said] What's the price of a pet canary? Some loose change, right? And God cares what happens to it even more than you do. He pays even greater attention to you, down to the last detail—even numbering the hairs on your head! So don't be intimidated by all this bully talk.
You're worth more than a million canaries.*
MATTHEW 10:29-31 MSG

*Oh yes, you shaped me first inside, then out;
you formed me in my mother's womb.
I thank you, High God—you're breathtaking!
Body and soul, I am marvelously made!
I worship in adoration—what a creation!*
PSALM 139:13-14 MSG

# . . . I will pray.

Dear Loving God,

Self-esteem problems are quite common. I remember facing them myself. The world can be ugly when you don't fit into a certain group's idea of what's perfect. Now I watch my daughter struggling with similar issues. She is not what she wants to be.

Lord, we all have flaws. Help my child to see that it is what is on the inside of a person that is the most important. Help her to minimize her weak areas and maximize her most positive qualities. I want her to see herself as You and I do, handcrafted by You in Your very image. I want her to know that her worth does not come from her looks or the clothes she wears. Her worth comes from belonging to You—from being a good, loving, kind person.

Help her to see beyond herself—to seek Your approval for who she is and what she does. Let her know, Father, that You love her beyond her comprehension. She is worthy because of who she has chosen to be on the inside.

Thank You, Father, that You do love us. Help my child to see that Your approval is all she really needs.

Amen.

A healthy self-image is seeing yourself as God sees
you—no more and no less.

Josh McDowell

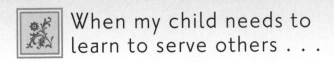

# When my child needs to learn to serve others . . .

[Jesus said] Whoever wishes to be great among you
must be your servant, and whoever wishes to be first among
you must be your slave; just as the Son of Man came not to
be served but to serve, and to give his life a ransom for many.

MATTHEW 20:26-28 NRSV

[Jesus said] Worship the Lord your God, and only him.
Serve him with absolute single-heartedness.

MATTHEW 4:10 MSG

Use your freedom to serve one another in love;
that's how freedom grows.

GALATIANS 5:13 MSG

All of you serve each other with humble spirits,
for God gives special blessings to those who are humble.

1 PETER 5:5 TLB

❀

Serve the LORD with gladness.

PSALM 100:2 KJV

# . . . I will pray.

Dear Lord,

Serving You means serving others—I know that, but it's not so easy to get that through to my child. Help me teach my child to begin to think of others first, before her own interests and priorities. Help me also to impress on her that when she serves others, she is serving You.

I know her behavior depends to some extent on what she sees me doing. So, Lord, help me to be a good example by reaching out to others and putting others before myself, not in a selfish, phony way—but serving from my heart.

I also ask that You show us opportunities to serve others together. I know it is important for her to see how fulfilling it can be to provide the answer to someone else's prayer or see someone succeed because you helped.

Thank You, Lord, for teaching us to serve others through Your incomparable gift. You didn't flinch at laying down all You had to come to our rescue. You sent Your own precious Son to give us hope and bring us back into relationship with You. Give me and my child that kind of serving heart.

Amen.

> In God's family there is to be one great body
> of people: servants. In fact, that's the way to
> the top in his kingdom.
>
> Charles R. Swindoll

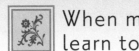# When my child needs to learn to share . . .

*Command them to do good, to be rich in good deeds,*
*and to be generous and willing to share. In this way*
*they will lay up treasure for themselves as a*
*firm foundation for the coming age.*
1 TIMOTHY 6:18-19

✿

*The wicked borrows, and cannot pay back,*
*but the righteous is generous and gives.*
PSALM 37:21 RSV

✿

*Generous people will be blessed,*
*because they share their food with the poor.*
PROVERBS 22:9 NCV

✿

*The world of the generous gets larger and larger. . . .*
*The one who blesses others is abundantly blessed.*
PROVERBS 11:24-25 MSG

# . . . I will pray.

Dear Father,

Sharing seems like such a basic skill, but teaching my child to open his clenched fists is one of the biggest challenges I've had to face so far. I've talked to him, coaxed him, scolded him, and read him every story I can think of that has to do with sharing. I've even read him verses from the Bible, but he still seems to have a death grip on his possessions.

Lord, some of the other moms say this isn't such a big deal—but I think it is. How can he ever share his thoughts, his burdens, his heart with You if he can't even share his possessions with those he says he loves? I believe sharing is one of the most important lessons my child needs to learn.

Show me how to approach this issue with him, Lord. Give me wisdom and courage to keep putting the principle out there. Then, I ask that You would do what only You can do: open my child's heart to this concept. Show him that there's freedom in release, hope in surrender. Thank You, Lord.

Amen.

Giving is a joy if we do it in the right spirit. It all depends on whether we think of it as "What can I spare?" or as "What can I share?"

Esther York Burkholder

# When my child needs strength . . .

*Have you not heard?*
*The everlasting God, the* LORD,
*The Creator of the ends of the earth,*
*Neither faints nor is weary. . . .*
*He gives power to the weak,*
*And to those who have no might He increases strength.*
*Even the youths shall faint and be weary,*
*And the young men shall utterly fall,*
*But those who wait on the* LORD
*Shall renew their strength;*
*They shall mount up with wings like eagles,*
*They shall run and not be weary,*
*They shall walk and not faint.*
ISAIAH 40:28-31 NKJV

*I delight in weaknesses, in insults, in hardships,*
*in persecutions, in difficulties.*
*For when I am weak, then I am strong.*
2 CORINTHIANS 12:10

*God is our refuge and strength,*
*always ready to help in times of trouble.*
PSALM 46:1 NLT

# . . . I will pray.

Precious Lord,

I know what it's like to feel as if you have no strength left. It's hard to go on. I've always dealt with weakness by calling on You—but my child doesn't yet understand how to do that.

Lord, lift her up into Your arms. Bear her weakness as Your own. Give her strength day to day when she feels her own is gone. Help her to make it through these next few days with a courage she never knew she had. And be there to comfort her in the days ahead.

I pray that the experience she is going through right now will set a new pattern for her life. I pray that she will learn to lean on You, to draw her strength from You, to understand how much You love and care for her. Knowing You as her Burden-Bearer will give her a source of real strength for every situation she will face.

Oh, Father, thank You for being strong when we are weak! Thank You that we can rest in Your strength and do not have to rely on our own.

Amen.

When a man has no strength, if he leans on God,
he becomes powerful.

Dwight Lyman Moody

# When my child is stressed out . . .

As pressure and stress bear down on me,
I find joy in your commands.

PSALM 119:143 NLT

The LORD will give strength to His people;
The LORD will bless His people with peace.

PSALM 29:11 NASB

Great peace have those who love thy law;
nothing can make them stumble.

PSALM 119:165 RSV

All your children will be taught by the LORD,
and they will have much peace.

ISAIAH 54:13 NCV

[ Jesus said] I have spoken to you, that in Me you may have
peace. In the world you will have tribulation; but be of good
cheer, I have overcome the world.

JOHN 16:33 NKJV

# . . . I will pray.

Loving Father,

Stress is taking its toll on my child. Her body and mind are reacting to the overload. She doesn't know how to say no or when to accept less than perfection. I fear that one of these days, Father, she may actually make herself seriously ill.

Please, Lord, give her peace. Help me teach her how to relax and spend time in Your presence in order to be refreshed. Teach her how to meditate upon Your Word and draw nourishment and energy from it. She needs to know that she does not have to do everything, nor does she have to be perfect. The world is not hers to carry.

I pray, Father, that she would leave her burdens at Your feet and not pick them up again.

Touch her body and mind and give her rest in You. Help her to be calm, settle her nerves. My prayer for her is peace within, Lord, the kind that only You can give. Spread that peace around her like a soft, warm cloak, Father. Thank You for showing us how to turn off the stress switch.

Amen.

Peace rules the day when Christ rules the mind.

Author Unknown

# When my child encounters violence . . .

*You have been my protection,*
*like a strong tower against my enemies.*
PSALM 61:3 NCV

*In God (I will praise His word),*
*In the LORD (I will praise His word),*
*In God I have put my trust;*
*I will not be afraid.*
*What can man do to me?*
PSALM 56:10-11 NKJV

*The Lord is faithful, and He will strengthen and*
*protect you from the evil one.*
2 THESSALONIANS 3:3 NASB

*The violence of the wicked will destroy them,*
*because they refuse to do what is right.*
PROVERBS 21:7 NCV

# . . . I will pray.

Dear Father,

My son came home yesterday a mess—a typical sign of a fight. I have never understood bullies, Lord, and I especially don't now. I have tried to teach my child that fighting isn't the answer. He can avoid dealing with people in anger. But I don't know what to tell him when he's being targeted day after day.

Lord, put a hedge of protection around him. Keep him safe as he goes to and from school. Help him to understand that these boys do not represent the majority of people he will encounter in life. Make him see that violence is never the answer. And even though he may have to stop and defend himself, Father, forgiveness is still needed.

Give me wisdom to deal with this situation. Show me how to calm his fears. And, Lord, if I have to speak with these boys' parents, let my words be words of life rather than words of condemnation and judgment.

Thank You for being a shelter when troubles brew and my child is affected. May he always seek You first when turmoil comes his way.

Amen.

Your response to a vicious assault can instantly reveal the Christian values by which you live.

James C. Dobson

# When my child needs wisdom . . .

*The profit of wisdom is better than silver, and her wages are better than gold. Wisdom is more precious than rubies; nothing you desire can compare with her. She offers you life in her right hand, and riches and honor in her left.*
PROVERBS 3:14-16 NLT

*I will bless the Lord who counsels me; he gives me wisdom in the night. He tells me what to do.*
PSALM 16:7 TLB

*I delight far more in what you tell me about living than in gathering a pile of riches. I ponder every morsel of wisdom from you.*
PSALM 119:14-15 MSG

*Train me well in your deep wisdom. Help me understand these things inside and out.*
PSALM 119:26-27 MSG

# . . . I will pray.

Dear Wise God,

My child has some tough decisions to make today, and I'm asking You to give him Your counsel. Believe me, advice is flowing freely from his friends and family members, but I know Your wisdom is perfect and theirs is not. I also know that whatever he decides, he will have to live with that choice for a long time. It needs to be right.

Lord, continue to tug at his spirit until he has considered what You have to say on the matter. Lay it upon his heart to spend time studying Your Word and talking this out with You in prayer. You have said that all we need to do is ask and You will give wisdom.

Give him peace if what he decides goes against what others think he should do, realizing that You see the future with clarity and purpose. Thank You, Father, for being all we need for every situation.

Amen.

❖

Knowledge is horizontal.
Wisdom is vertical—it comes down from above.

Billy Graham

# When my child needs help dealing with classmates . . .

*You bless the righteous, O LORD;*
*you cover them with favor as with a shield.*
PSALM 5:12 NRSV

*Do not let kindness and truth leave you;*
*Bind them around your neck,*
*Write them on the tablet of your heart.*
*So you will find favor and good repute*
*In the sight of God and man.*
PROVERBS 3:3-4 NASB

*Whoever loves pure thoughts and kind words*
*will have even the king as a friend.*
PROVERBS 22:11 NCV

*The child grew up healthy and strong.*
*He was filled with wisdom beyond his years,*
*and God placed his special favor upon him.*
LUKE 2:40 NLT

# . . . I will pray.

Caring Father,

I look back on my own school years and think of all the fun I had with my friends. We were so young and carefree. I also remember not fitting in some days, the disappointment of not being part of the "in" group and the hurt of being teased.

I wish I could shield my child from all that. I would love for her to remember only the fun, friendships, and thrill of learning new things. But I can't. Help her, Lord, to look past the hurtful kids—to smile when she is told her clothes are not the latest fashion, to spend time with the kids who are not the most popular, and to simply enjoy the good times.

It must have hurt You to see how Your Son was mocked during His time here on earth. He didn't fit in with the popular crowd either, Father. He looked beyond all of that and, in the process, was able to complete His mission to bring us salvation.

I know You can help my child do the same. Give me the right words to teach her to deal wisely with those who attend school with her. Make this time in her life a special one she will remember with pleasure.

Amen.

Anyone with a heart full of friendship has
a hard time finding enemies.

Author Unknown

# When my child needs help with an employer . . .

*Faithful messengers are as refreshing as snow in the heat of summer. They revive the spirit of their employer.*
PROVERBS 25:13 NLT

❁

*Workers who tend a fig tree are allowed to eat its fruit. In the same way, workers who protect their employer's interests will be rewarded.*
PROVERBS 27:18 NLT

❁

*Servants, respectfully obey your earthly masters but always with an eye to obeying the real master, Christ. Don't just do what you have to do to get by, but work heartily, as Christ's servants doing what God wants you to do. And work with a smile on your face, always keeping in mind that no matter who happens to be giving the orders, you're really serving God. Good work will get you good pay from the Master, regardless of whether you are slave or free.*
EPHESIANS 6:5-8 MSG

*Never slander a person to his employer. If you do, the person will curse you, and you will pay for it.*
PROVERBS 30:10 NLT

# . . . I will pray.

Loving Father,

It must be difficult to be the person who's in charge—dealing with deadlines, mistakes, weather, breakdowns, money problems, and an ever-changing work force. It must be hard for a boss to keep things in perspective and do what is right for the company while being fair to every employee.

My child is facing a situation at work right now. Most of the time, he doesn't know what his employer actually wants from him. It was another tough day at work for him today.

Lord, I pray that You would give him a calm spirit and peace of mind. Give him the strength and endurance to keep doing his best no matter the outcome. His hard work will pay off in the end. Maybe his boss will never notice but You see, Lord. You know how much effort he is making.

I also pray that my child's employer will feel Your presence in his life. Give him perspective, insight, and success as he does his job managing his employees. And thank You for bringing peace to this situation.

Amen.

Work should be looked upon, not as a necessary drudgery to be undergone for the purpose of making money, but as a way of life in which the nature of man should find its proper exercise and delight and so fulfill itself to the glory of God.

Dorothy L. Sayers

# When my child has concerns about friends . . .

*When others are happy, be happy with them.*
*If they are sad, share their sorrow.*
ROMANS 12:15 TLB

✿

*It's better to have a partner than go it alone.*
*Share the work, share the wealth.*
*And if one falls down, the other helps,*
*But if there's no one to help, tough! . . .*
*By yourself you're unprotected.*
*With a friend you can face the worst.*
*Can you round up a third?*
*A three-stranded rope isn't easily snapped.*
ECCLESIASTES 4:9-10,12 MSG

✿

*[Jesus said] This is my commandment, that you love one*
*another as I have loved you. No one has greater love than*
*this, to lay down one's life for one's friends.*
JOHN 15:12-13 NRSV

*Bear one another's burdens,*
*and thereby fulfill the law of Christ.*
GALATIANS 6:2 NASB

# . . . I will pray.

Dear Father,

Good friends are special, Lord. They mean so much to us and add such joy to our lives—especially when the friendship has lasted a long time. That's why the struggle my child's best friend is going through touches so close to home. When my child's friend hurts, she hurts. She doesn't always know what to say.

Father, give our child the wisdom to know when to speak words of comfort and when to simply be by her friend's side. She doesn't understand the why of it all—only that her friend is sad and confused. I pray that the love my child has would create a safe haven for her friend. That the friendship she bears would be enough to make up for losses at home some days.

Thank You, Father, for friends. For bringing them into our lives to share our secrets, burdens, and pleasures. Help my child to be a good friend, Father—a true and faithful friend indeed, just as You are.

Amen.

Friendship adds a brighter radiance to prosperity
and lightens the burden of adversity
by dividing and sharing it.

Author Unknown

# When my child's future is uncertain . . .

Trust in the LORD with all your heart
And do not lean on your own understanding.
In all your ways acknowledge Him,
And He will make your paths straight.

PROVERBS 3:5-6 NASB

✿

The path of the righteous is like the light of dawn,
which shines brighter and brighter until full day.

PROVERBS 4:18 RSV

✿

There is surely a future hope for you,
and your hope will not be cut off.

PROVERBS 23:18

✿

"I know the plans I have for you," says the LORD.
"They are plans for good and not for disaster, to give
you a future and a hope."

JEREMIAH 29:11 NLT

# . . . I will pray.

Dear Lord,

If we adults often find the future unsettling, how much more do our children. That's why I'm here before You today, Lord. Help my child find his way. One day he's certain he wants to do one thing, and then before I know it, he's changed his mind—again.

Father, I believe that he's struggling because he has not yet placed his future in Your hands. He's still caught up in his own ideas and interests. When his feelings change or he gets distracted by something new, all his resolve comes undone.

Guide my child to Your purpose, I pray. Show him Your plan for his life and place an excitement in his heart to go after it with his whole being. Only then will he be settled toward what lies before Him.

I pray also for myself, Lord. I don't want my own ideas and panic to cause him further confusion or instability. Help me to put my trust in You as well, knowing that You love my child and are even more committed to seeing him succeed than I. I hand my precious son over to You right now. Thank You, Lord.

Amen.

Never be afraid to trust an unknown future
to a known God.

Corrie ten Boom

# When my child is in trouble with the law . . .

*I urge, then, first of all, that requests, prayers,*
*intercession and thanksgiving be made for everyone—*
*for kings and all those in authority, that we may live peaceful*
*and quiet lives in all godliness and holiness. This is good,*
*and pleases God our Savior, who wants all men to be saved*
*and to come to a knowledge of the truth.*
1 TIMOTHY 2:1-4

*I call to God,*
*and the LORD saves me.*
*Evening, morning and noon*
*I cry out in distress,*
*and he hears my voice.*
PSALM 55:16-17

*God is a righteous judge.*
PSALM 7:11 NASB

*Righteousness and justice are the foundation of Your throne.*
PSALM 89:14 NASB

# . . . I will pray.

Precious Lord,

The police called again last night. Another trip to the station in the dark, both of us sick with worry, wondering what we would find this time. I honestly do not know how much more we can take. Days spent trying to imagine what is going on, nights spent crying out to You to keep him safe: When will it end? Why can't he see what he is doing not only to himself but to his family?

Oh, Father, give us wisdom. Restrain us from saving him every time he is in trouble. Place the right people in front of him, Lord—those who will help him see his mistakes. It's so hard to let him suffer the consequence of his actions.

I ask also that You would give us peace. You know exactly what we are going through. You know where he is even when we don't. I know You have everything under control, so help us to rest in that truth! We can't fix this, Lord, but You can! I thank You that he is forever in Your hand. Bring him home to us and to You, Father.

Amen.

Justice is nothing other than
love working out its problems.

Joseph Fletcher

# When my child's marriage is in danger . . .

*By wisdom a house is built,*
*and through understanding it is established;*
*through knowledge its rooms are filled*
*with rare and beautiful treasures.*

PROVERBS 24:3-4

*They shall be My people, and I will be their God;*
*then I will give them one heart and one way,*
*that they may fear Me forever, for the good of them*
*and their children after them.*

JEREMIAH 32:38-39 NKJV

*Submit to one another out of reverence for Christ. Wives,*
*submit to your husbands as to the Lord. For the husband is*
*the head of the wife as Christ is the head of the church, his*
*body, of which he is the Savior. Now as the church submits to*
*Christ, so also wives should submit to their husbands in*
*everything. Husbands, love your wives, just as Christ loved*
*the church and gave himself up for her. . . . Husbands ought*
*to love their wives as their own bodies. He who loves his wife*
*loves himself. After all, no one ever hated his own body, but*
*he feeds and cares for it, just as Christ does the church.*

EPHESIANS 5:21-25,28-29

# . . . I will pray.

Dear God,

I spent the evening worried about my precious child. It wasn't easy for me when he married. I wondered if they were old enough, mature enough, committed to You enough to make it. Now I'm more concerned than ever. Will they be able to see this marriage through, to make it a priority in their lives?

It's not that their problems are insurmountable, Lord, and they have assured me that there is still a strong love between them. But I hear the tension in my child's voice and feel the distance between the two of them when they're in my presence.

Lord, let them see what their marriage can be like if only they invite You into the equation. Help them to realize that it is not what she or he needs to change, but what they each need to surrender to You.

You are the great Reconciler, Lord. Step in now, I pray, before angry words cut wounds too deep to heal, before pride and discontent cause barriers too high to climb. Give them each a revival of heart and a revival of love—for You and for each other.

Amen.

A good marriage is not one where perfection reigns:
it is a relationship where a healthy perspective
overlooks a multitude of "unresolvables."

James C. Dobson

# When my child's religious instructors need wisdom . . .

*[Christ] is the one who gave these gifts to the church: the apostles, the prophets, the evangelists, and the pastors and teachers. Their responsibility is to equip God's people to do his work and build up the church, the body of Christ, until we come to such unity in our faith and knowledge of God's Son that we will be mature and full grown in the Lord, measuring up to the full stature of Christ.*

<small>EPHESIANS 4:11-13 NLT</small>

*The purpose of my instruction is that all the Christians there would be filled with love that comes from a pure heart, a clear conscience, and sincere faith.*

<small>1 TIMOTHY 1:5 NLT</small>

*Let the teaching of Christ live in you richly. Use all wisdom to teach and instruct each other by singing psalms, hymns, and spiritual songs with thankfulness in your hearts to God.*

<small>COLOSSIANS 3:16 NCV</small>

*And now, friends, we ask you to honor those leaders who work so hard for you, who have been given the responsibility of urging and guiding you along in your obedience. Overwhelm them with appreciation and love!*

<small>1 THESSALONIANS 5:12 MSG</small>

# . . . I will pray.

Heavenly Father,

This is a tough world we live in. It would be easy for people to just huddle up at home with their own families, but so many caring people reach out selflessly—those who have taken upon themselves the responsibility for my child's religious education, for example.

Oh, I know, Lord, that first and foremost that falls to me, but I'm so grateful for the help of these dedicated people. They multiply my effectiveness and clarify where my own teaching is weak. Thank You for placing them in my child's life, Lord.

Give wisdom and guidance to these teachers. I pray that they would seek Your face and spend time with You before each class. Give them answers for the tough questions, Lord, and more insight and understanding than they ever imagined possible. Show me how to work with them to provide a unified message to our children.

Bless them, Father—these tireless servants of Yours. And make me sensitive to the needs in their lives, asking that You watch over their lives just as they are watching over the lives of others.

Amen.

A teacher affects eternity;
he can never tell where his influence stops.

Henry Gardiner Adams

# When my child is unhappy about being single . . .

*I wish that all were as I myself am. But each has a particular gift from God, one having one kind and another a different kind. To the unmarried and the widows I say that it is well for them to remain unmarried as I am.*

1 CORINTHIANS 7:7-8 NRSV

*Turn to me and be gracious to me,
for I am lonely and afflicted.
Relieve the troubles of my heart,
and bring me out of my distress.*

PSALM 25:16-17 NRSV

*God has said, "I will never, never fail you nor forsake you."*

HEBREWS 13:5 TLB

*[Jesus said] Surely I am with you always,
to the very end of the age.*

MATTHEW 28:20

# . . . I will pray.

Dear Lord,

Another wedding invitation arrived in the mail. It seems a wedding is taking place every time we turn around these days. The problem is the questions our daughter must face when she attends her friends' weddings.

"Are you dating anyone?" "When are you going to settle down?" They don't mean to hurt her, Lord. She wants that special someone in her life too. She wants a family and a home.

Father, give her patience to wait upon Your timing, to rejoice in her singleness. She can do wonderful things while she is on her own. She can get her education behind her, serve You in ways she cannot once she is married. I pray for peace in her heart. May You be the One who fills her very being. Let her not be lonely.

Thank You, Lord, for being husband, wife, father, or mother to all of us. Thank You for loving her more than a husband ever could. I believe You have someone special for her. But if being single serves Your purposes in her life, let her understand You are all she needs.

Amen.

There is never a place in the Bible where it says that marriage makes you happy. It says over and over again that God makes you happy.

Dick Purnell

# When my child's teachers need wisdom and encouragement . . .

*I pray that out of his glorious riches he may strengthen you*
*with power through his Spirit in your inner being.*
EPHESIANS 3:16

❀

*You desire truth in the inward being;*
*therefore teach me wisdom in my secret heart.*
PSALM 51:6 NRSV

❀

*She opens her mouth with wisdom,*
*and the teaching of kindness is on her tongue.*
PROVERBS 31:26 RSV

❀

*Encourage one another and build up each other,*
*as indeed you are doing.*
1 THESSALONIANS 5:11 NRSV

❀

*Men who encourage the upright to do good*
*shall be given a worthwhile reward.*
PROVERBS 28:10 TLB

# . . . I will pray.

Precious Lord,

Thank You for my children's teachers. They work hard to make their classrooms places where children can feel safe and learn to their hearts' content. I appreciate what they do for all of our children, but especially for those who belong to me.

Teaching must be unusually difficult some days. Most teachers are dealing with fewer resources than they need to get the job done, while others find themselves unable to help when they face the problems today's kids must grapple with.

Lord, encourage those teachers who have been assigned to my child. Give each one a megadose of guidance, joy, insight, kindness, stamina, and creativity. Help them to impart to their students not just knowledge but a love of learning that will last a lifetime.

I pray that You will enable them to do their best, know that what they do is appreciated, and receive encouragement from knowing that You see their giving hearts. Bless them with students who want to learn.

Thank You for those who spend themselves on behalf of others. Bless them with a loving relationship with the greatest Teacher of all—Your Son, Jesus Christ.

Amen.

The mediocre teacher tells. The good teacher explains. The superior teacher demonstrates. The great teacher inspires.

William A. Ward

# When the world my child
# lives in becomes chaotic . . .

The LORD is God, and he created the heavens and earth and
put everything in place. He made the world to be lived in,
not to be a place of empty chaos.
ISAIAH 45:18 NLT

When the country is in chaos,
everybody has a plan to fix it—But it takes a leader
of real understanding to straighten things out.
PROVERBS 28:2 MSG

[God says] I'm creating new heavens and a new earth.
All the earlier troubles, chaos, and pain
are things of the past, to be forgotten.
Look ahead with joy.
Anticipate what I'm creating.
ISAIAH 65:17-18 MSG

God is a safe place to hide, ready to help when we need him.
We stand fearless at the cliff-edge of doom,
courageous in seastorm and earthquake,
Before the rush and roar of oceans,
the tremors that shift mountains.
Jacob-wrestling God fights for us,
GOD-of-Angel-Armies protects us.
PSALM 46:1-3 MSG

# . . I will pray.

Wonderful Lord,

The world is changing, evolving. Just when I think I know what's going on, I am surprised again by the latest development. But I'm not afraid, Lord. No matter how chaotic, how extreme, how confusing things get, You will always be right by my side. What concerns me is my child.

After all, Lord, she doesn't have years of experience following You. She hasn't yet experienced Your utter faithfulness on her behalf. Oh, sure, she's seen You move in her life, but she's still young—she hasn't experienced the long-term security that comes from knowing You.

That's just the reason that I bring her before You today. Give her a clear perspective on what is going on in this world of hers. Teach her to find peace where there is no peace—by trusting You. Help her to find joy where there is no joy—by trusting You. Help her to discover love where there is no love—by taking Your hand. I know, Lord, that in Your presence, she will find safety and peace.

Amen.

If the basis of peace is God,
the secret of peace is trust.

J. N. Figgis